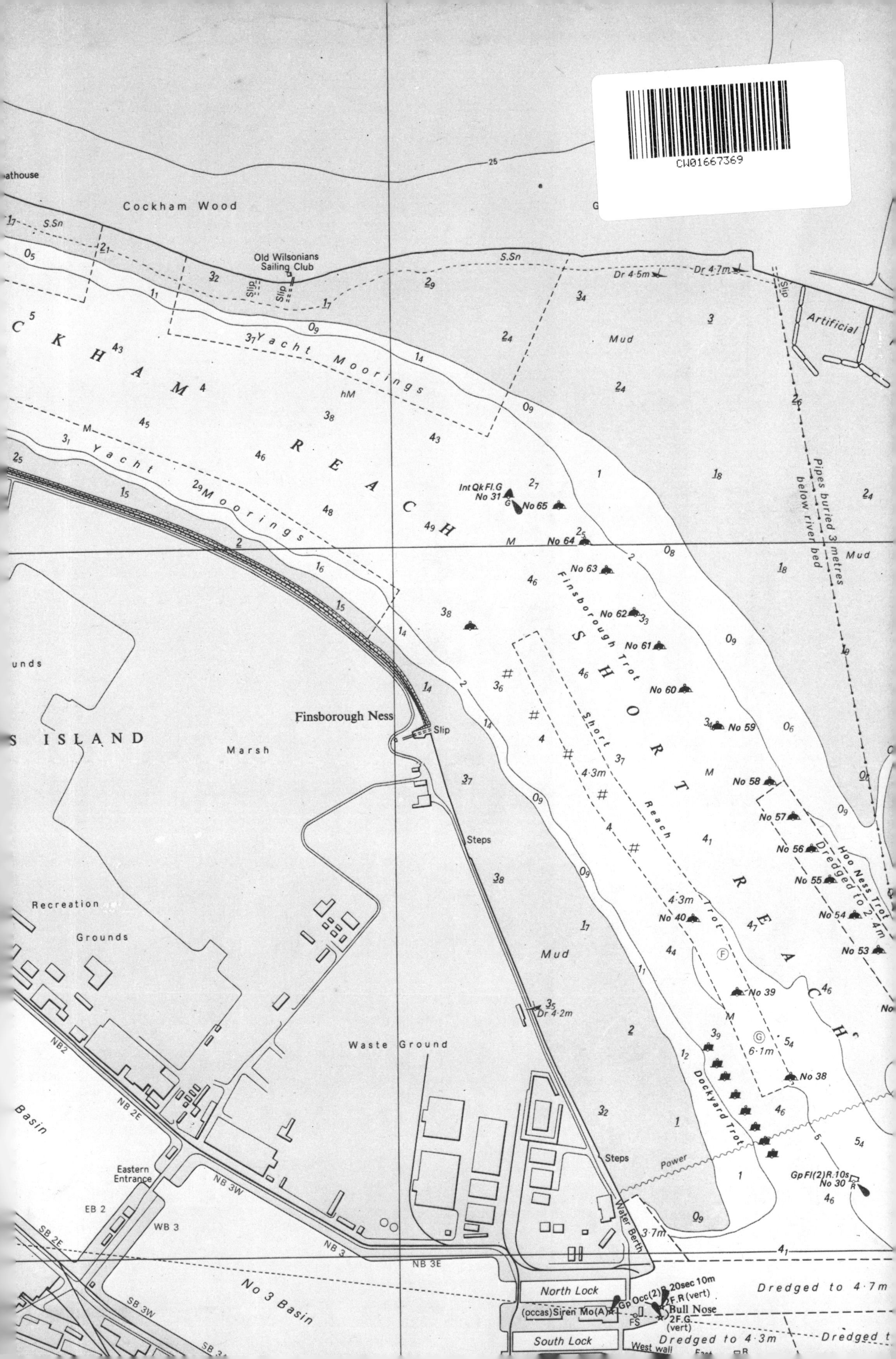

Cockham Wood
Old Wilsonians Sailing Club
Slip
S.Sn
Dr 4·5m
Dr 4·7m
Artificial
Yacht Moorings
Mud
hM
COCKHAM REACH
Pipes buried 3 metres below river bed
Int Qk Fl.G
No 31
No 65
No 64
No 63
No 62
No 61
No 60
No 59
No 58
No 57
No 56
No 55
No 54
No 53
No 40
No 39
No 38
No 30
Gp Fl(2) R.10s
Finsborough Trot
Short Reach Trot
Hoo Ness Trot
Dockyard Trot
SHORT REACH
Dredged to 2·4m
4·3m
6·1m
Finsborough Ness
S ISLAND
Marsh
Steps
Dr 4·2m
Recreation Grounds
Waste Ground
Power
Water Berth
3·7m
Eastern Entrance
Basin
No 3 Basin
NB2
NB 2E
NB 3W
NB 3
NB 3E
EB 2
WB 3
SB 2E
SB 3W
North Lock
South Lock
(occas) Siren Mo(A)
Gp Occ(2) R 20sec 10m
2F.R (vert)
Bull Nose
2F.G (vert)
FS
West wall
Dredged to 4·7m
Dredged to 4·3m

£3=

MEDWAY YACHT CLUB

The first hundred years

1880-1980

W. L. WYLLIE, A.R.A., celebrated marine artist and enthusiastic yachtsman. Club Commodore 1896-1904.

MEDWAY YACHT CLUB

the first hundred years
1880-1980

COMPILED BY DON ELLIS

Publishers:
SOUTH EASTERN MAGAZINES LTD.,
MAIDSTONE. 1979

First published 1979

ISBN standard edition 0 900893 08 7

ISBN de luxe edition 0 900893 09 5

Printed by South Eastern Newspapers, New Hythe Lane, Larkfield, Kent
Bound by W. & J. Mackay Ltd., of Chatham

Foreword

by the Rt. Hon. Edward Heath, M.B.E., M.P.

TOGETHER with all the sailing fraternity I would like to offer my warmest congratulations to the Medway Yacht Club on its Centenary in March 1980.

No one will have to be reminded of the distinguished part which the Medway has played in British history over many centuries. Nor will the citizens of Chatham and Rochester require to be told of the vital importance of Chatham Dockyard both to the town and to the county in former times.

Least of all will we in Kent need to have it explained to us that it is the Medway which separates Men of Kent from Kentish Men. That is all part of history.

And now the Medway Yacht Club, created in more recent times, has become part of that history too; but the living history of today.

This book eloquently describes the life of the river, its institutions and its club. Starting first to meet in local hostelries, the club first established its own headquarters at Rochester in a wooden clubhouse on the Esplanade.

continued overleaf

Today, it has fine buildings and an excellent hard down river from Upnor, with a large membership not only from the local towns and villages but to a considerable extent from London itself.

I first made use of the club's facilities ten years ago. While racing on a Saturday afternoon my Fireball Blue Heather II capsized in a blow off Dumpton Gap and, while drifting towards Broadstairs Jetty, damaged its mast.

I was determined to race the following day and to enable me to do so the local distributors agreed to bring a new mast as far as the Medway Yacht Club if I were to collect it from there.

When I arrived, everyone at the club was most helpful and I managed to get the new mast back to Broadstairs in time for the second race of the weekend.

The first Morning Cloud, a 34 foot Sparkman & Stephens design, was built on the Medway and launched in March 1969 from the Royal Engineers' Pier. Afterwards we celebrated in the club house.

At the end of a good season's racing, both on the East Coast and the Solent, I shipped her out to Australia where we won the Sydney to Hobart Race at the end of 1969.

For me the Medway Yacht Club holds these very pleasant memories. For its members they will be many times more numerous. The pleasure which the Club has given both to those who race and those who cruise is incalculable.

All those who have enjoyed its facilities owe a great debt to its Flag Officers and to the members of its committee, who have contributed so much to its success over past years.

The future of the club will be even more splendid than its past. I wish the best of fortune to all those who sail from it.

Contents

Men at the helm

THIS book marks the centenary of the Medway Yacht Club, founded in 1880. Appended is a list of the men who in the course of those 100 years have served the club in the role of Commodore.

1880	*W. H. Nicholson*
1881	*Maj. J. Fellowes, R.E.*
1882-1883	*Maj. W. H. Roberts*
1884	*J. Hulkes*
1885-1889	*Capt. J. du T. Bogle, R.E.*
1890-1895	*C. Arkoll*
1896-1904	*W. L. Wyllie, A.R.A.*
1905	*W. J. Goldsmith*
1906-1907	*Morton W. Smith*
1908-1929	*C. Willis, J.P.*
1930	*E. B. Willis*
1931	*J. Paxton*
1932-1935	*F. C. B. Baldwin*
1936	*T. C. Spurway*
1937-1939	*T. G. Galbraith*
1946-1947	*F. Parham*
1948-1949	*Norman West*
1950-1952	*W. V. Price*
1953-1955	*Max Hamilton*
1956	*J. W. Field*
1957-1958	*Harold A. Dyer*
1959-1960	*D. S. Clarabut, D.S.C.*
1961	*R. R. Clifford*
1962-1963	*M. P. O. English*
1964	*R. Mellor*
1965-1966	*Cmdr. G. S. Clarabut, D.S.O., D.S.C.*
1967-1968	*S. W. J. Smith*
1969-1970	*Dr. A. T. Rogers*
1971-1972	*F. R. Crossley*
1973-1974	*R. P. Townshend*
1975-1976	*Dr. S. J. Cox*
1977-1978	*P. N. Harvey*
1979-	*N. P. Steele*

IT IS a great honour for me, as Commodore during Centenary Year, to introduce this book. If we could go back in time to 1880 how proud our founders would have been if they could have known that we would be celebrating our one hundredth birthday this year. The Club owes them all a great debt of gratitude.

Our thanks are also due in great measure to the thirty-two previous commodores and all their willing helpers who have made the MEDWAY YACHT CLUB what it is today. *Long may it continue!*

PETER STEELE

Introduction

THE RIVER Medway, we suppose, could well be described as the "little brother" of its near neighbour, Old Father Thames.

But not all the glamour and romance that is associated with Britain's most famous waterway can dim the fact that the lesser known Medway has greater naval and maritime traditions than even London River — the Thames. As local historian James Presnail wrote in his memorable book, "The Story of Chatham": "My purpose has been the telling of the story of a town which can proudly lay claim to having been the birth-place of the Royal Navy."

A proud claim indeed, and one founded on the fact that the very first warship of the Royal Navy as we know it today, the Great Harry, was reputedly built at Chatham, on the Medway, in 1488. And from that day onwards, Presnail tells us, "Chatham has continued its honourable association with the Royal Navy."

It is only right, however, to point out that there are those who would have it that the Great Harry was built, not at Chatham but, in fact, at Woolwich.

But for the purposes of this book we have taken the word of our own local scribe, James Presnail, and leave it to history to determine the rights and wrongs of this particular argument.

Chatham still has its Royal Dockyard, albeit the sails and timbers of the Great Harry and her like, have given way to the more mysterious and, some would say, sinister intricacies of the nuclear submarine, with which the Dockyard and a large part of its workforce are now concerned.

Sir Francis Drake spent many of his boyhood days on the Medway at Upnor and Gillingham.
By courtesy of the National Maritime Museum, London.

But to return to the building of the Harry. A century or so later, in the reign of Queen Elizabeth the First (Good Queen Bess), the dockyard workers at Chatham, under the orders and direction of Sir John Hawkins, were to repair and service the ships that later sailed out to destroy the Spanish Armada.

Sir Francis Drake who, with Hawkins and Raleigh, was to play such notable part in the destruction of the Spanish Fleet, was one of two great English naval heroes who learned their early seamanship on the tidal waters of the Medway.

Drake's father, the Rev. Edmund Drake, was instituted vicar of Upchurch near Gillingham in 1560, and Francis is said to have lived with his father in a naval ship, one of many that had been transferred from Portsmouth to Gillingham.

The young Drake was then aged about 7 and, while he may have been born at Tavistock, in Devon, there is no doubt that what might be termed his early apprenticeship to the ways of ships and the sea was served among a variety of ill-assorted tutors on the waters of the Medway, off Gillingham and Upnor.

The other, and perhaps even more illustrious English naval hero who spent his early formative years on the Medway, was, of course, Horatio, Lord Nelson, the victor of Trafalgar.

Nelson, as a boy of 12, was, we are told, for some reason "found wandering alone in the streets of Chatham, until noticed by an officer who put him aboard his uncle's ship, the Raisonable". There, at Queen's Stairs, Presnail tells us, Nelson "learnt the rudiments of his noble profession."

From Nelson, of course, it is but a short step to that most famous of all British fighting ships, H.M.S. Victory, in which he was to win immortality at the Battle of Trafalgar.

Nelson's early association with the Medway make it fitting that Victory should have been built at Chatham. She was laid down in 1759, but not launched until May 7th, 1765.

For 13 years she remained in the Medway and must have been seen by the young Nelson when he joined

Lord Nelson — an early association with Chatham and the Medway. Courtesy of the National Portrait Gallery.

Raisonable in January 1771. It was not until April 1803, however, following a somewhat chequered seagoing career and having been largely rebuilt, that Victory became Nelson's flagship.

On October 21st 1805, off Cape Trafalgar, the combined fleets of France and Spain were vanquished. Lord Nelson, as we know, was mortally wounded, and joy at the victory was compounded with sorrow at his death in the final moments of his greatest triumph.

H.M.S. Victory now stands, triumphantly, a few yards inside the main gate of Portsmouth Dockyard, a proud memorial to Britain's naval history and, of course, a very big tourist attraction. Some people might say that Chatham and the Medway should have provided the last resting place for this great ship!

A less memorable moment in the history of the Medway, from the British point of view, that is, occurred in June 1667, when a Dutch fleet under the command of Admiral de Ruyter, sailed up the river and attacked English naval ships, burning

H.M.S. Victory — built on the Medway at Chatham, birth-place of the Royal Navy.

three and capturing a fourth.

It was the first time a hostile fleet had sailed up the Thames or Medway since the days of the Vikings. The humiliation it caused can well be imagined.

The Dutch have, of course, sailed up the Medway on many subsequent occasions and in all manner of vessels, but with a difference; they now come with the hand of friendship instead of with sword and fire!

Naturally there is another aspect of the Medway, other than its association with the Royal Navy and acts of warfare. We refer to its commercial side, largely centred on the busy port of Rochester.

Ships of all nations ply up and down the river, transporting all manner of varying cargoes. The annual volume of trade involved is considerable.

Lastly, but by no means least, the Medway provides an outlet for those who, to use a time-honoured phrase, enjoy "mucking about in boats". Especially sailing boats.

Which is where the Medway Yacht Club comes in, and what this centenary book is all about. Read on......

Charles II — Father of English yachting. Courtesy of the National Portrait Gallery.

CHAPTER ONE

How it all began

WE ARE indebted to Chatham Dockyard for the fact that "the now popular sport of yachting" was unknown in England prior to 1660.

Charles II when in exile in Holland, it is said, became acquainted with yachts, where they were in use as a means of transport for high officials of state and "for the sport of racing". When Charles was recalled to the throne of England, he used a Dutch Admiralty yacht to take him to the English ships sent to Holland to accompany him home.

He was so enamoured of the yacht, which he had used on previous occasions, that he told the Burgomaster of Amsterdam he would have a similar vessel built when he arrived in England, for use on the Thames. The Burgomaster replied that he would, in fact, present the King with a yacht recently built in Amsterdam, and this vessel, suitably embellished, was sent to England.

The King accepted the gift but later commanded Peter Pett, then Commissioner of the navy at Chatham, and his brother Christopher Pett, Master Shipwright at Woolwich, each to build a yacht. That built by Peter was named after the Queen, the Katherine.

They were not, however, the sort of yachts we know and sail today. The Katherine, for instance, had a keel of 49 feet, a tonnage of 94, a crew of 30, and carried eight three pounder guns. What a stir a yacht like that would cause on the Medway today!

That great diarist and man of the Navy, Samuel Pepys, is said to have recorded on May 21st, 1661: "So took barge again and was overtaken by the King in his barge, he having been down the river with his yacht this day for pleasure to try it, and as I hear, Commissioner Pett's do prove better than the Dutch one and that his brother built."

King Charles II had many other yachts built, the most famous being the Fubbs, built by Phineas Pett, (son of Peter), later made Commissioner of the Navy and knighted in 1680. The Fubbs differed from the previous yachts in that she was ketch rigged, that is fitted with two masts and a bowsprit, with yards and square sails on the main mast and a square topsail and lateen sail on the mizzen mast.

The Fubb's rig, coupled with her design, made her faster in sailing than the other yachts. "This exceptional speed", it is recorded, "combined with the picturesque painting and delicate carved work that enriched her, drew marked attention and caused her to become very popular with ship lovers of the nation and thus added more laurels to Pett's crown of renown as a shipbuilder."

From all of which it would seem that Charles II could well be described as the Father of English yachting, aided and abetted, of course, by the Pett family, Peter, Christopher and Phineas.

CHAPTER TWO

The first years

"The Medway, close to London, is a wonderful spot for sailing. The River winds and turns and gives a test on all points of sailing, no matter what direction the wind is blowing."

(The Uffa Fox Book of Sailing)

STRANGE as it may seem, little or nothing appears either to have been recorded or, if so, retained regarding the manner in which the Medway Yacht Club actually came into being. Meetings and discussions must have taken place, of course, but if minutes of these were, in fact, taken at the time, they are not, alas, among the otherwise voluminous records of the club's activities so faithfully compiled after the M.Y.C. had established itself following the official formation on March 11th, 1880.

That a new club on the Medway was being proposed is, however, recorded in minutes of the Royal Engineers' Yacht Club, which had already been established at Upnor several years earlier. In 1879, the Sappers were discussing whether they should support the proposed newcomers to the sailing waters of the Medway and, we quote, "the feeling of the meeting was taken on the subject and perfect satisfaction appeared to be expressed."

This feeling of satisfaction towards the newcomers was later reflected in the appointment of Major J. Fellowes, R.E., as Commodore of the M.Y.C., in its second year. The Commodore in the inaugural year of 1880, was a civilian, Mr. W. H. Nicholson.

The new club quickly established itself and earned what in those days must have been the highly coveted recognition of Hunt's Yachting Magazine. In the 1880 handsomely bound volume of the magazine, Hunt's reported the first race of "this newly-formed Club", on Wednesday, June 1st, and observed that "the committee may be congratulated on the excellent entries." Further races in this inaugural year were also reported on by Hunt's.

In those early years, and indeed for many more to follow, the club was established up river at Rochester. The membership was naturally somewhat on the small side, numerically speaking, and possibly a trifle exclusive compared with

W. L. Wyllie's sketches evoke the Medway of 1898

Gaff yawl 'Armorel' (29 tons T.M.) on the club listings from 1909-19

modern standards. That the members enjoyed themselves, both on the river and at their social occasions ashore, goes without saying.

For social get-togethers, and indeed for their committee meetings in those early days, the club appear to have distributed their patronage among the better-known hostelries of the district, such as the Bull Hotel, and King's Head, Rochester, and the Sun Hotel at Chatham.

Numbered among the club's many distinguished Flag Officers is that famous marine artist W. L. Wyllie, A.R.A., who held the office of Commodore from 1896-1904. On Tuesday, March 8th, 1898, he not only presided over a Grand Smoking Concert held by the Medway United Aquatic Clubs at the Sun Hotel, but also illustrated the original programme of the event with some of his delightful pen and ink studies of ships and boats on the Medway.

From its title, the Medway United Aquatic Clubs would appear to have been a conglomeration of all the many clubs associated with the river at that time. Its modern counterpart is the Medway Yachting Association, which is responsible for organising the annual Medway Regatta, of which more anon.

As we have said, membership in those early days was on the small and rather exclusive side. An early year book, that for 1894, records just 86 members. Today, the club boasts something like 1,300 members. Of these, some 600 are full members, the remainder being made up of associates, juniors and cadets.

Of those 86 members listed in 1894, many were well-known names in and around the Medway Towns. names such as C. Arkcoll, T. L. Aveling, Lord C. Beresford, F. C. Boucher, R. F. Brain, H. J. and H. M. Cobb, W. D. Driver, E. A. Gill, W. Haymen, A. E. Kidwell, R. J. Passby, H. E. Prall, C. Willis and, of course, W. L. Wyllie, among others.

Lord Charles Beresford was a name to become well known in naval circles and his address at this time, 1894, was listed as H.M. Dockyard, Chatham.

CHAPTER THREE

The Medway Kittiwakes

THE OBJECTS OF THE CLASS

Are to enable yachting men, whose means do not admit of their building a new "rater" every year, to race in a class of boats of one design, in which comfort and economy are not wholly sacrificed to speed.

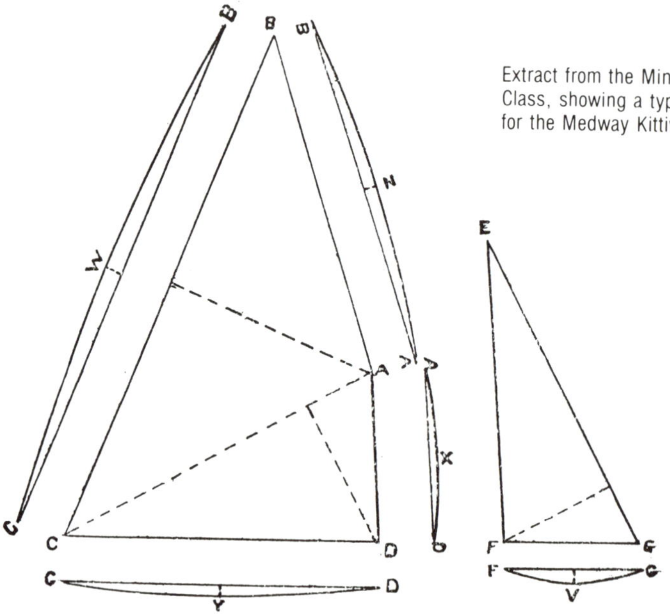

Extract from the Minute Book of Class, showing a typical sail layout for the Medway Kittiwakes.

THE BOATS sailed by members in those early days were of a varied nature and design. In that first race in June, 1880, for instance, Hunt's reported that most of the entries were cutters. There were also a couple of yawls and a schooner.

Great interest appears to have been taken in the locally built 5 ton cutter Hilda, owned by Mr. A. B. Horsnaill, and the yawl Little Sally (Mr. T. Aveling Jnr.), "whose sailing qualities were as good as ever". To Hilda went the distinction of being first over the finishing line.

Some years later, on October 20th, 1897, a meeting took place at the King's Head Hotel, Rochester, that was to be quite a landmark (or should it be seamark?) in the history of the club. It had been called "to discuss the formation of a one-design class on the river Medway for the coming season."

There was much talk on the subject and various plans, models and specifications were described and on show. Among them were those relating to the Gravesend class boats, which were fully explained by the designer, Mr. G. R. Larnder. Backing him was Mr. Herbert Winder, captain of the Gravesend Sailing Club, who "gave his experience of the results of the racing of the Gravesend boats extending over three seasons."

Eventually, on the proposition of

Mr. Charles Willis, Jnr., who proposed the formation of the Medway One Design Class, soon known as the Medway Kittiwakes.

Mr. Charles Willis, Jnr., seconded by Mr. H. J. Cobb, it was unanimously decided to form a one-design class of boats on the Medway to be called, not surprisingly, The Medway One-Design Class.

Several of those present expressed their willingness to build, but the decision as to which type of boat should be adopted was deferred to a further meeting called for a week later.

This duly took place, again at the King's Head, on October 27th, when there was further discussion as to the merits of designs that had been advocated by their various sponsors. Members had, however, obviously been impressed by what they had

Three men in a boat. One of the club's early Kittiwakes, pictured in full sail.

heard and seen regarding the Gravesend class of boat and eventually it was unanimously adopted.

Mr. A. L. Oswald was elected secretary of the new class and Mr. Larnder generously allowed his design, model and specification to be used free for the first batch of the new boats to be ordered for the Medway.

He further extended his generosity by agreeing to periodically inspect the boats built locally, also free of charge. Such is the camaraderie existing among sailing clubs.

But back to the new one-design boats. Headquarters for the class were established at the King's Head. A succession of meetings followed, at which matters for deliberation included such items as class rules, tenders for construction and a suitable name for the class as a whole.

Among names put forward for consideration were White Wings, Seagulls and just plain Match Class. None of these met with general favour.

Then came a suggestion from the Gravesend Club that Medway should identify with them by adopting one common title. The Thames and Medway Kittiwakes Class.

The kindness of the Gravesend club in allowing Medway to adopt their design was, naturally, much appreciated, but it was pointed out that Medway boats were to be carvel built rather than clinker, and for that reason could not be so closely identified with Gravesend. Also, Gravesend were a club, whereas Medway would be adopting a class within a club.

As a tribute to the part Gravesend had played in helping to establish the new class it was, however, decided that it should henceforth be known as The Medway Kittiwakes.

The objects of the new class were clearly defined as follows: "To enable yachting men whose means do not admit of their building a new 'rater' every year to race in a class of boats of one design in which comfort and economy are not wholly sacrificed to speed."

Class rules were also drawn up; one of which, it is interesting to note, was to the effect that "when racing, the limit of the crew shall be three, all of whom shall be bona fide amateurs."

By the end of the year, the headquarters of the Medway Kittiwakes had been switched to the Bull Hotel, where the charge for the hire of a room for committee meetings would, it seems, result in an annual saving of one guinea, no mean sum in those days!

In the following year, 1898, the Kittiwakes were in full sail, so to speak, and five of them were listed to compete in a class race at a Medway Yacht Week programme of events. Mr. W. L. Wyllie's Pensee Fugitive was first over the finishing line to claim a first prize valued at £1.10 shillings.

Other Kittiwakes of the time bore such names as Mimosa, Scallywag, Roli Poli San, Minicoy and, naturally, Kittiwake.

The Kittiwakes were to continue sailing for 15 seasons, until 1912, by which time they had been reduced to just two. Their end as Medway's one-design class boat was near and eventually hastened by the outbreak of the First World War in 1914. Competitive sailing naturally ceased during the war years, as was again to happen when war came in 1939.

CHAPTER FOUR

England v. Australia

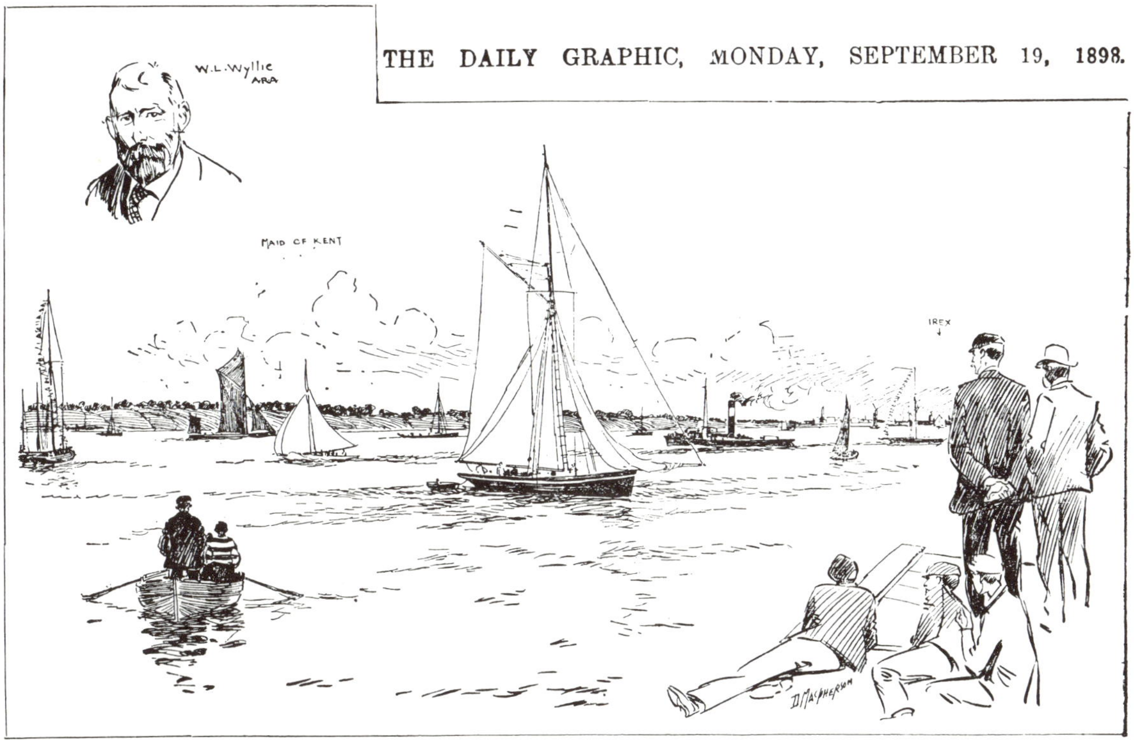

THE ANGLO-AUSTRALIAN BOAT SAILING RACE: SATURDAY'S MATCH BETWEEN THE MAID OF KENT AND THE IREX ON THE MEDWAY.

IN THE summer of 1898 the eyes of the yachting world became focused on the River Medway. Mr. Mark Foy, Commodore of the Australian Flying Squadron in Sydney had brought his boat Irex to England. Although 12 years old, the Irex had beaten all-comers Down Under and Mr. Foy conceived the idea of coming over to challenge the yachtsmen of this country.

The challenge was at once taken up by Commodore W. L. Wyllie, on behalf of the Medway Yacht Club, and the prospect of an England versus Australia sailing match on the tidal waters of the Medway caught the imagination of the sporting public over a very wide field of interest, both national and international.

The Times, Pall Mall Gazette, Daily Graphic, Daily Mail, The Referee, The People, Yachting World, The Field and other publications of the day devoted columns of space to the races and to the events leading up to them. The local Press of the time, the Chatham and Rochester Observer and the Chatham and Rochester News, also gave the matter the attention and prominence it so obviously merited.

Time was not on the side of the Medway Club. Mr. Foy had his boat. Mr. Wyllie had still to produce a suitable challenger, but not for nothing did one notable journal of the time describe him as "the celebrated marine artist and father of yachting on the Medway". He called a meeting at the Bull Hotel and formed a syndicate to build a boat designed by Wyllie himself and Mr. Linton Hope.

Construction was assigned to Messrs. Gill and Sons, the Rochester barge owners and builders, and in

ENGLAND v. AUSTRALIA

THE INTERNATIONAL MATCHES ON THE MEDWAY

THE first of the series of five international matches between the *Maid of Kent*, owned by a syndicate headed by Mr. W. L. Wyllie, A.R.A., and representing the Medway Yacht Club, and the *Irex*, owned by Mr. Mark Foy, and representing the Sydney Flying Squadron, of which organisation Mr. Foy is the Commodore, will take place on the Medway on Saturday. The dates fixed for the remaining races of the series are September 19th, 21st, 23rd, and 24th. The course for Saturday's match is from Gillingham Reach, down to and round a buoy off Port Victoria, and back to the starting-line. The course for the remaining matches will not be fixed until after the conclusion of the first race.

MRS. W. L. WYLLIE
Will Steer the *Maid of Kent*

HOW THE MATCH WAS ARRANGED

Early in the present year Mr. Mark Foy, who is engaged in London in business, had the *Irex* brought over from Sydney on the *Persian Gulf* with the idea of sailing her in a few matches on this side before his return to Sydney next year. Being without information as to the best mode of racing against English boats, he naturally enough asked for enlightenment on the subject, and discovered that there was no class here against which the *Irex* could be pitted. The dimensions of the Australian boat having been given, Mr. W. L. Wyllie, A.R.A., was soon in the field with an offer to build a British boat to meet the Antipodean in a series of international matches. Conditions were agreed upon without any difficulty being experienced, the English boat being allowed to add to the length what excess the *Irex* had in beam, there being an understanding that there should be no time allowance on either side. Mr. Foy, on being called upon, furnished the following figures as the dimensions of the *Irex*, which, by the way, has proved herself to be the best boat of her class in Sydney harbour :—Length, 22ft. ; beam, 9ft. ; depth, 2ft. 6in. She is a centreboard open-decked craft having a fin of 7ft. drop and an overall length, from end of bowsprit to end of boom of about 60ft. A meeting was held under the auspices of the Medway Yacht Club to consider Mr. Foy's proposals, and on the motion of Mr. Wyllie it was agreed to form a syndicate to build a boat to race against the *Irex*. The result was the *Maid of Kent*, which was built by Messrs. Gill & Son, of Rochester, to the design of Mr. Linton Hope. She is a 24-footer with a very slight overhang, a nice powerful boat well adapted as a rival for the Antipodean craft. She has a length of 24ft. over all, 22ft. on the water-line, and a beam of 7ft. 7in. The illustration we give is from a photo of the *Maid of Kent* by Mr. J. J. Eastmead, of Rochester, taken just after being launched from Messrs. Gill's yard, with a full crew of seven on board, the number which will race. Mrs. Wyllie is at the helm. It will be seen that the boat has a very low freeboard; stability being obtained by the great breadth and by the crew all sitting out as far as possible to windward. The cockpit is only 6in. below the decks, sloping down toward the centreboard case, so that the boat is an entirely watertight shell, and any water coming over in a heavy sea will either find its way down through the slot in which the centreboard works, or roll out to leeward. It is needless to say that, as in the case of the Australian boat, the crew have no chance of keeping themselves dry. Althoug h, as will be seen from the photo, the mast looks a great length, and the yard of the lug stands up 12ft. above the mast, the boat has proved to be very stiff, and carries her canvas well in a stiff breeze. She appears to be very fast, and she simply loses the new Medway Kittiwakes, either on or off the wind. She has also had a short trial with the crack 24-footers *Chittabob* and *Hochelaga*, and easily ran by them to leeward, and although her sails were not fully stretched, she also beat them handsomely to windward. Built entirely of cedar, the *Maid of Kent* has a sail area of between 500 and 600ft., but against this has to be placed the *Irex's* spread of close upon 1,000ft. The Committee of the syndicate consists of Mr. W. L. Wyllie, A.R.A., Mr. Charles Willis, jun. (Rear-commodore Medway Yacht Club), Mr. T. L. Aveling, Mr. H. Burton, Mr. E. J. Goldsmith (Rear-commodore Thames Estuary Cruising Club), Mr. J. E. Castle, Mr. G. R. Larnder, and Mr. A. L. Oswald.

MR. W. L. WYLLIE, A.R.A.,
Head of the Syndicate owning the *Maid of Kent*

MR. MARK FOY INTERVIEWED

Mr. Foy went down to Burnham on Thursday last, and set about drilling his crew for the matches. A meeting was held in London a few days ago, attended by a large number of

Facsimile page from The Yachting World, September 1898.

Australian yachtsmen now located in this country and anxious to form the crew of the *Irex*. A number were selected and duly turned up on the Crouch for a trial spin last week, at the conclusion of which Mr. Foy was interviewed by a representative of The Yachting World.

"I am very well satisfied with the way the boat is sailing," said Mr. Foy, "considering the scratch nature of the crew I have got together. Of course, we are not doing anything like our best, as nearly the whole of the men on board are strange to the craft, besides which we have had to augment our numbers by shipping a few local hands to make up a respectable complement."

"Are you perfectly satisfied with the conditions under which the matches will be sailed?"

"I would have preferred a number of the races being sailed at Burnham as I think the course there an excellent one, but I cannot say anything about the Medway course, as I have not had a chance yet of seeing it. Mr. Wyllie, however, shows himself totally averse to sailing anywhere but on the Medway, and as he has the right under the conditions to insist upon the races being held there, I suppose there is no use saying anything more about the matter."

"What do you think of the chances of the respective boats in the match?"

"At first I was very sanguine that the *Irex* would be able to hold her own, but I may say that when I brought her over here I never for a moment contemplated that it would be necessary to build a brand new boat to meet her. Then again it seems that I made a mistake of something over one foot in giving the beam of the *Irex*, which has enabled the Medway boat to be built rather longer on the water line than she should be. The mistake was entirely my own, so that I am solely to blame, and I can have no redress whatever, as one of the conditions of the match is that there shall be no time allowance to either boat."

"What conditions will suit your boat best in the matches?"

"Well, we want a good steady breeze like we have had to-day, but we must also have smooth water to sail in. As you will have seen to-day the boat ships a good quantity of water over the side. The match, however, is a sporting one, and the only thing I have to add is that I hope the best boat may win."

HOW TO VIEW THE RACE

Very complete arrangements have been made for the matches. On Saturday the Medway Steam Packet Company are running a steamer to follow the boats round the course. The steamer will leave Strood Pier at 10.15, calling at Chatham at 10.30. The trains to catch the steamer are :—8.45 a.m. from Charing Cross to Strood, arriving there at 9.57 a.m., and Victoria 8.30 a.m. to Chatham, arriving there at 9.20 a.m. Applications for tickets should be made to the Secretary, Medway Steam Packet Company, Acorn Wharf, Rochester.

Maid of Kent *Photo by* Mr. J. J. Eastmead, *Rochester*

CLUB NEWS

ALEXANDRA YACHT CLUB

The race for cruisers, postponed from the 27th ult., was sailed on Saturday, at Southend, the course being from the Pierhead, round the Nore lightship, and the Jenken buoy, leaving both on the starboard hand, and finish at the starting-point. The entries were :—*Amy*, Mr. E. Pennell, scratch; *Kittiwake*, Messrs. Coombe and Macnaughten, 3m.; *Siola*, Dr. Jowitt, 30m.; and *Cigarette*, Mr. P. J. Russell, 20m. Mr. F. Greenfield was the officer of the day, and got them off at 11.45, wind westerly. After a very even start *Amy* soon established a powerful lead, and won at 2h. 4m. 20s., beating *Kittiwake* on the handicap by 19 minutes.

BURNHAM YACHT CLUB

On Saturday this club held two races, the first being for vessels of 5 tons and over, starting at 12.45, and the second for vessels under 5 tons T.M., starting at 3.15. In the first race *Maimuna* and *Minkie* were first away, *Gondola*, unfortunately, gybing and smashing her spinnaker boom just after gunfire. The course was round W. Buxey buoy, 18 miles, for £5, presented by Mr. E. Runchman, and second, £1. 10s., and third, 10s., by the club. *Gondola* was first home, gaining on the turn to windward back from the Buxey in the W.N.W. wind. All carried jackyarders. The finishing times were :—*Consuelo* (second prize), Dr. Robinson, 4h. 17m. 32s.; *Nona*, Mr. L. R. Higgins, 4h. 9m. 50s.; *Maimuna*, Mr. A. Hassall, 4h. 6m. 21s.; *Gondola*, Mr. M. Thompson, 4h. 5m. 16s.; *Yanell* (first prize, Mr. B. Russell, 4h. 22m. 15s.; *Minkie*, Mr. W. J. Nicholls, 4h. 29m. 55s. *Gondola* was scratch, giving *Maimuna* 4m., *Nona* 7m., *Consuelo* 22m., *Yanell* 29m., and *Minkie* 32m. The smaller craft were sent two rounds of the Roach course in W.N.W. wind, light to finish. This race was a sweepstake of 7s. 6d. each, with £1 added by Mr. S. Haynes, and given for professionals at helm. *Soprano*, Mr. S. Haynes, at scratch, took first prize; *Theo*, Dr. Downman, second, with 8m.; *Wild Duck*, Mr. J. E. Matthews, third, with 12m.

Facsimile page from The Yachting World, September 1898.

exactly a month they were, to quote a national publication of the day, to turn out "a splendid specimen of English craftsmanship". The boat was named Maid of Kent and she was ceremoniously christened by Mrs. Wyllie.

Not only did she christen the Maid, but Mrs. Wyllie was to go on to skipper her to overwhelming victory over the Australian challenger.

As the Sydney Daily Telegraph wryly observed: "The result was fully expected by Sydney sailing men, none of whom expected anything else under the circumstances. Irex is an old boat . . . the crew can hardly have been experienced boat-sailers, and

Irex, the challenger.

Mr. Foy, who sailed his own craft, is not by any means an expert. The fact that a lady (Mrs. Wyllie) was at the tiller of the English craft only goes to show that those interested did not over-estimate the chances of the Sydney boat."

The challenge match between Irex and Maid of Kent was to have been decided by the best of five races for the Anglo-Australian Shield, jointly provided by Mr. Foy and the Medway syndicate. The course was from Gillingham Pier, round the Stone Bank buoy and back to Gillingham, leaving the Folly Gas buoy to port and the Stoke Shoal buoy to starboard. The races were due to be sailed on September 17th, 19th, 21st, 23rd and 24th.

But Irex was no match for Mrs. Wyllie and The Maid, the English boat gaining three successive victories all by the most convincing margins, thus rendering it unnecessary to complete the series of five.

As the Chatham Observer said in its leader column: "The Medway has shown itself able both to build and to race. The contest between our local yachtsmen and the Australians has excited an enormous amount of interest in the yachting world, and it is to the credit of our river that it has carried the honours in a well contested race, which was entered into and carried through by both parties in a most sportsmanlike spirit."

Mr. Foy indeed proved a good and generous loser, readily conceding that on the day the Maid had proved the better boat. It is obvious, however, that he considered that conditions on the Medway had not favoured his boat, and he later made desperate attempts to obtain a second, or return, match.

This time, however, the Australian wanted the races to be sailed on

A tense moment for Irex crew members, with the Maid on her bows.

Southampton Water. To this the Medway club could not agree, pointing out to Mr. Foy that the conditions for the original match had stipulated that the races should be sailed on the Medway. It was also stressed that in all challenge matches the holders of any trophy involved had the right to defend it on their own waters.

From the correspondence that ensued between Mr. Foy and the Medway club it is obvious that the M.Y.C. were quite prepared to race again in 1899, but only on the Medway.

The unhappy Mr. Foy made it clear, however, that Australian boats "cannot compete on strong tides", and there was never any chance that his hopes for a second series of races could then be realised.

The victorious Maid of Kent under way.

CHAPTER FIVE

Sailing on smooth water

THE CLUB'S progress towards and into the 20th Century continued slowly, surely, but largely unspectacularly. All that appeared to ruffle the otherwise smooth water on which it was then sailing, both metaphorically and literally speaking, seems to have been the occasional protest arising between members during the course of racing.

One such protest, involving the Kittiwake boats Mimosa and Preciosa in 1904, was given most lengthy and serious consideration by the club committee. In a few words, Preciosa had fouled Mimosa's middle with her bowsprit during a Sweepstake Handicap race. Each blamed the other, Preciosa relying on Y.R.A. rule 31 and Mimosa countering with Y.R.A. rule 29.

The first meeting was adjourned without decision but at the resumed hearing it was decided that Mimosa was solely to blame for what had transpired between the two boats. Even then it was agreed to send the case to the Yacht Racing Association for their consideration, and, hopefully, confirmation.

A month later, it is recorded, came the following reply from Y.R.A. headquarters at Ryde: "Dear Sir, Mimosa v Preciosa. I beg to inform you that in this case the Council has decided that the decision of the (M.Y.C.) Committee be upheld. Yours faithfully, B. Heckstall Smith, Secretary."

The wisdom and justice of the Medway club had been completely vindicated by the highest authority in the yachting world of racing.

Although the headquarters of the club was still listed as Rochester, much of the racing, including the annual regatta, took place down river at Upnor. A barge, and sometimes a tent, were hired and fitted out to do the honours as regatta headquarters.

It is also recorded that a special boat would often be hired from a Mr. Elliott to run from Sun Pier, Chatham, to Upnor, "for the convenience of members and friends going to the annual regatta at Cockham Woods."

There is an interesting note concerning the 1904 regatta, or Medway Week, as it was called. The minutes show that "the hon. secretary was desired to write and think Mrs.Wyllie for her kind offer to be 'at home' to members and friends during the week to lunch, and also to accept her kind offer to provide tent, tables, chairs, servants, plate, linen and glass, and the hon. secretary was left to make arrangements to send down tea and whisky and soda for the members and friends each day."

Needless to say there was a lot of activity of a more serious and strenuously competitive nature out on the river itself during the course of a long programme or racing. But it does show what genuinely happy occasions those old-time regattas were, lacking as they did the more sophisticated facilities that obtain today.

The Mrs. Wyllie referred to was, of course, the wife of Commodore W. L. Wyllie, and the same Mrs. Wyllie who had steered Maid of Kent to victory over the Australian boat Irex a few years earlier. The Wyllies lived at Hoo Lodge, just above Upnor. What happy, halcyon sailing days they must have been!

In 1906, the committee was obviously concerned with the idea of providing a suitable clubhouse. But where? Commodore Morton Smith was "very doubtful" about taking up a proposed scheme for a clubhouse above the bridge.

This, he felt, would make Medway an up-river club "instead of one in which something bigger than Kittiwakes were encouraged." Eventually, a sub-committee was set up "to make enquiries at Upnor and Cockham Woods, and see what can be done to find suitable quarters in that neighbourhood."

The first tentative step had been taken in the eventual complete move to Upnor that was to follow nearly half-a-century later.

Even before the Great War, eyes were turned down river to Upnor and beyond, as a possible sight for a permanent club house.

CHAPTER SIX

Out of the blue

IN APRIL 1910, there came, right out of the blue, so to speak, a cablegram from Australia. It read: "Sydney Flying Squadron challenges race September this year for Anglo-Australian Shield."

The Medway Club, under Commodore Charles Willis, was quick to respond, but not before it had checked back on the conditions which had governed the original match in 1898. Further conditions were subsequently drawn up to govern all or any future contests.

These latter, it will be remembered, Mr. Mark Foy the Sydney club's Commodore, had found himself unable to accept, which had seemed to put an end to the prospect of any further matches between the two clubs. But here, some 12 years later, Mr. Foy appeared to be spoiling for another fight, and Medway was quick to take up the challenge.

Back went the following cablegram: "Accept challenge subject immediate cable confirmation races to take place on Medway under original conditions." Mr. Foy was not slow to respond. "I confirm your cable, will race under original conditions on Medway in September."

All seemed set for a belated and quite unexpected return match between Medway and the Sydney Flying Squad. Or did it? A copy of the conditions signed by officers of the Medway club was despatched for counter-signing by the Australians. A sub-committee was set up by Medway to consider the question of providing a suitable boat for the proposed re-match.

It was decided to ask Mr. Wyllie, who was now living at Portsmouth, if he would allow the original Maid of Kent, of which he was the owner, to be used in eliminating trials or in the proposed races themselves.

It was further agreed that if a new boat became necessary, the design should be entrusted to Mr. Linton Hope, co-designer with Mr. Wyllie of The Maid. Possible improvements to the Maid were also considered.

Difficulties, however, arose concerning the possible release of The Maid by Mr. Wyllie and it was decided to ask Mr. Linton Hope to prepare a provisional design of a boat "to defend the shield."

Here it should be pointed out that one of the race conditions stated: "The crews to be amateurs; the challenger to be allowed a professional pilot who shall not touch the tiller."

Late May brought this further cablegram from the Sydney Flying Squadron: "Conditions arrived. Our club no amateur definition. Intend sending old club members as skippers and crew. Await reply before signing."

The Medway club's reaction to this was to send all the correspondence on the matter, together with a copy of the conditions, to the Yacht Racing Association for their opinion. The Sydney Flying Squadron, informed of this decision, promptly cabled back as follows: "Cannot wait. Accept old members or withdraw. Reply immediately. Sydney."

The cables continued to hum. Back went this reply from Medway:

Alderman Charles Willis, J.P., C.C., the club's longest serving Commodore (1908-1929).

"Original conditions specify amateur crews. Regret cannot recede." In July came this cable via Mr. Foy's London business office: "Tell Medway postpone race next season. Arrive London August discuss."

Whether or not Mr. Foy actually came to London is not revealed and the next we hear of the matter is dated January 1911 when Mr. Foy is reported as challenging for races to take place in the following September, "the conditions to be the same as those which governed the last series of races."

Medway, however, would then appear to be getting just a little bit tired of the whole thing. They replied that they were not disposed to spend money on building a new boat "of a perfectly useless type such as the Maid of Kent was."

They would, however, be prepared to meet the Australians in a series of matches in a 6 or 7 metre boat, I.Y.R.A., which would overcome the difficulty respecting the manning of the Australian boat. International rules, it seemed, provided for a number of amateurs and professionals in each class.

Just how the Australians reacted to this is not recorded. What is clear is that there was no second trial of sailing strength between the two clubs.

One day, perhaps, there will come another challenge from Australia, somewhat on the lines of the more famously known America's Cup races.

If such a challenge should materialise, one thing is for certain; a boat today will cost far, far more than the modest £200 or so outlay on the Maid of Kent back in the halcyon days of 1898. And could such a boat now be designed, built, rigged and ready to sail, all within the space of six weeks as it then was? It makes you think!

Not that the matter of England v Australia had entirely ended. It was brought to light again more than half a century later and in a most unusual way.

In 1950, an article appeared in a local newspaper concerning Mr. E. A. Gill, whose family had been closely connected with the Medway Yacht Club and whose firm had, of course, built the Maid of Kent for the England v Australia races in 1898. Mr. Gill had also been a member of Mrs. Wyllie's triumphant crew in the races.

Following publication of the 1950 newspaper article referred to, Mr. Gill received an interesting letter from a Mr. W. J. Tallamy of Gillingham. He wrote: "I have a shield described as 'Anglo-Australian Challenge Shield', bearing the flags of Medway Yacht Club and Sydney Flying Squadron........ Does it have anything to do with the Maid of Kent in which you raced?"

Mr. Gill passed this letter on to the Medway Yacht Club and wrote: "I have no knowledge of this Shield. The only one I know of was that designed by Mr. Wyllie and I believe that is now resting in Sydney."

Which is all very strange. The rules governing the England v Australia races in 1898 clearly stated: "The shield shall not be won outright by any club and shall only be held in trust by any club winning it, until such time as it is challenged for and won by another club, which club shall hold it for the time being on the same conditions."

Mr. Foy certainly did not win the shield, but it is known that he had said he would greatly like to take it with him on his return to Australia! Perhaps it was indeed presented to him as a good loser!

What of the shield mentioned by Mr. Tallamy? Was it indeed the original trophy, or perhaps just a replica! Nobody really seems to know. At least the challenge shield is not in the possession of the Medway Yacht Club, to whom it should apparently belong!

CHAPTER SEVEN

The long wait

Warships in Short Reach, site of many M.Y.C. races long before the clubhouse moved down from Rochester.

BY 1913, committee meetings were being held at the Castle Club, Rochester, overlooking the river near the bridge.

In July of that year the Commander-in-Chief, The Nore, Admiral Sir Richard Poore, advised the committee that "as the warships would be away on manoeuvres during July, he could suggest no date for the ships' boats' race."

It was decided that Commodore Charles Willis should try to see Sir Richard personally on the matter and suggest a date at the end of September. Whether, in fact, that meeting, or the race itself, ever took place, is not revealed. War, of course, was fast approaching.

The next significant date recorded in the club minutes is April 15th, 1914, when the annual general meeting was held at the Castle Club. At this a vote of thanks was recorded to Mr. Norman Burns, who had resigned as secretary "on leaving the district to take up an appointment in London."

Mr. Desmond Tonks was elected secretary and treasurer and Mr. Willis was reappointed Commodore. But it was to be almost five years before Mr. Willis was to sign the minutes of that April 1914, A.G.M. as being a true record of what had transpired.

The signing took place at a further annual meeting held on February 13th, 1919 at 280 High Street, Rochester, at which Mr. Willis was confirmed in office as Commodore.

What had transpired between those two dates was the great War, 1914-18, although no reference to it is actually made in the minutes! Mr. G. G. Watson became the new secretary and treasurer, and no fewer than 32 new members were elected at that first post-Great War meeting.

The club was off to a good and confident resumption of activities.

A few months' later the club sent three of its members to have talks with the Gravesend club. The object — "to ascertain a few particulars with the idea of formulating rules etc., when the club should have a clubhouse."

Things moved quickly after this. The City Council was asked to lease the club a plot of ground in Willis Avenue, leading down to the water's edge and a subscription list was launched for the provision of a clubhouse building.

Commodore Charles Willis started the ball rolling with a donation of £50 and others followed with smaller sums. In no time at all £150 had been promised, and it was decided to canvass for further financial support of the project.

What had often been talked about now seemed to be "taking real form", as one member put it.

The real form duly materialised in the shape of a timber building from Westgate-on-Sea, purchased at a cost of £275 and eventually moved and established on the land leased by the club from the City Council.

A committee meeting held at 280 High Street, Rochester, on March 15th, 1920, heard a report on progress regarding removal of the building from Westgate. The next committee meeting, on April 8th, was held at — the clubhouse. Progress indeed!

CHAPTER EIGHT

The new jewels

The Pearl. One of the club's early Medway One-Design boats, which became known as the Medway jewels.

THE YEAR 1921 signalled the end of the old Kittiwakes and the emergence in their place of a new one-design class. The Kittiwakes had provided good sport for 15 seasons but by now were reduced to just two boats and there had been no class racing since the Great War.

Both Commodore Charles Willis and Vice-Commodore H. J. Cobb expressed themselves keen to start a new one-design class on the Medway, and this wish coincided with news that Sea View Mermaids, at the Isle of Wight, were desirous of selling their seven one-design boats.

Negotiations were soon in hand and eventually resulted in the seven boats being bought as they lay at the Isle of Wight for a total of £630, or £90 each. That was in October 1921.

In the spring of the following year the boats were towed to Portsmouth and put on rail to Strood Dock, where they arrived on April 3rd 1922, and were put in the water next day. The individual charge for bringing the miniature fleet to Strood was £14.14s.8d., raising the cost of each boat to £104.14s.8d.

It was decided that they should be known as the Medway One-Design Class, operate under the rules of the old Kittiwakes, and be named after gems or precious stones. Mr. A. L. Oswald, who had been secretary of the Kittiwakes, was elected captain of the new class.

Among the names allocated to the newcomers were Jade, Crystal, Sapphire, Emerald, Pearl, Ruby and Onyx. Commander H. P. Wilson, R.N., donated a silver challenge cup to be competed for by the new class, which was thereby well and truly launched.

CHAPTER NINE

Shot in the arm

Shot cartridges supplied, instead of blanks...

THAT it was not always plain sailing, so to speak for the club, was highlighted by a dramatic and most unfortunate incident that occurred in the 1920's.

Medway had been asked by the Leigh Yacht Club to time in a race the Essex club was sailing from Leigh to Cockham Woods, Upnor. To this Medway readily agreed, and also to hold a smoking concert for the visitors after the race, the finish of which was, however, marred by an unusual and most unhappy occurrence.

It appears that shot cartridges instead of blanks were supplied by a local firm and what this led to is described in the club minutes of the day as follows: "A child, Blanche Mould, employed by Mr. Barton, the manager of Brice's Tea Gardens at Cockham Woods, was accidentally shot in the arm, three shots having grazed off the brushwood in front of the firing station."

The consternation that ensued can well be imagined. The child was "immediately attended by Dr. Wall, and the hon. secretary made a statement to the village constable."

The club was also quick to inform the firm that supplied the cartridges that they would be held responsible for all claims in respect of the accident, including the doctor's bill!

There is no further mention of the incident in the club records, so it can be hopefully assumed that young Blanche Mould came to no permanent or serious harm. But someone, somewhere, must surely have "got a rocket" over it.

At about the same time another matter of some importance was engaging the attention of the Medway club and its members. This was no less than the suggested absorption of, or merger with, the adjoining Rochester Cruising Club.

There was considerable discussion and correspondence on the matter and eventually a special general meeting of the yacht club was called to consider a motion to the effect that members of the cruising club should be elected members of the yacht club, en bloc.

All to no avail. The motion was defeated by 24 votes to 15. So it was sailing as usual for the M.Y.C. members.

A boat party adds to its cheer with the traditional 'cuppa'.

Club membership increased considerably during the inter-war years.

CHAPTER TEN

Coming and going

THAT the acquisition of the new clubhouse was most popular with members is made clear in the committee minutes compiled at the time. Improvements and structural alterations and repairs were carried out from time to time and a bar, complete with steward, was installed.

Billiards, whist drives and smoking concerts were much in vogue and members from visiting clubs were also able to enjoy the social facilities provided.

Changes in the overall membership were obviously taking place all the time, with new members being enrolled in what would appear to have been more than sufficient numbers to fill the gaps caused by resignations, mostly due to the members concerned leaving the district.

One such loss obviously much regretted was that of Major R. G. R. Hunter, R.E. Elected a member on February 21st, 1923, he was appointed Rear Commodore just over a year later, on March 21st, 1924.

Alas! Only a few months later, in September, Major Hunter was reporting that he had been ordered to Ireland. The club placed on record its very high appreciation of the services he had rendered to the club and adding that by his removal from the district "the club loses a member they hold in the highest esteem as a true sportsman."

It later appeared that the gallant major's departure to Ireland may have been delayed by an attack of appendicitis, but the fact remained that the club had lost a popular Rear Commodore. But four years later Major Hunter was back and became the winner of the season's one-design class and later still was elected to the sailing committee.

Among the newcomers elected to the club at round about this time is to be found the name of Mr. Donald Maxwell, the well-known Kent author and artist, who at the time was living at The Beacon, Borstal Road, Rochester.

Another interesting note records that the committee, in 1926, supported a resolution by the National Defence League, calling for the abolition of the use of pit ponies!

It should not be assumed that sailing and racing on the river was not also engaging the active attention of members. It was, and full programmes were at all times being arranged by the committee.

A very colourful nautical character was numbered among the guests at the club's annual dinner at the Bull Hotel, in November 1928. He was listed as Capt. Drake ("the lone sea rover").

Capt. Drake, it seems, had sailed single-handed across the Atlantic. He told members and guests that he preferred sailing single handed on deep water. His last trip had lasted three years and five months and he had encountered rocks, sandbanks, and "almost every obstacle imaginable."

He was then waiting for a new boat in which to sail to the Pacific. His previous boat, the Pilgrim, was

The annual dinner at the Bull Hotel at the time of Capt Drake's exploits.

lost when it struck a sandbank, he said.

Some sailor, Capt. Drake, and no wonder, with such an illustrious nautical name to live up to. He must surely have been one of the first of the lone, long distance sailors.

In the following year, 1929, Mr. Charles Willis, who had gone to live at St. Leonard's, intimated that he would not be seeking re-election as Commodore, a role he had filled since 1908. This news was received with the utmost regret and many were the tributes paid to his long and distinguished service to the club.

But the name Willis was, in fact, to continue in the role of Commodore, for at the 50th annual meeting of the club, in what was its Jubilee Year, Mr. E. Basset Willis was elected to the office. He had previously held the rank of Vice Commodore.

At the club's Jubilee dinner it was disclosed that they had 34 boats afloat and a membership of 99, figures which "compared favourably with those of any other club in the kingdom."

CHAPTER ELEVEN

A vexed question

M.Y.C. boats moored alongside for an album photograph. Moorings at this time were becoming a matter of some concern.

THE QUESTION of moorings is one that always excites the interest of all yachtsmen. There are never enough of them. That is certainly the case today, when the club has over 200 moorings at Upnor, and a waiting list that never seems to get any shorter.

Moorings also engaged the attention of the club in quite a big way in 1933, when members called for a special meeting on the subject. News that the Motor Boat Association had applied to the local council for 50 permanent moorings was obviously a matter for concern and the word "protest" was much in the air.

The club invited the Mayor, Deputy Mayor and Town Clerk to attend the meeting and hear the club's views on the matter. The Town Clerk confirmed that the city council had agreed to provide the moorings and to charge £100 for 15 years. It was thought that number would be sufficient for all demands.

The club view was that the Medway Conservancy Board should take

A panorama of the Medway, showing clearly the demand for moorings.

charge of and allocate all moorings.

This, in fact, seems to have been done, with the Conservancy Board allocating 18 moorings to the club and 45 to the M.B.A., "to be operated by them on behalf of members of the Association and of non-members." And that, it was recorded, was the final decision of the Board.

It probably did not please the yachtsmen, but nevertheless had to be accepted. To help deal with what was obviously a somewhat delicate situation it was decided to appoint a moorings sub-committee and to formulate a frame of general rules for the satisfactory handling of the moorings question.

The suggestion was also made that a standing committee of members of all the Medway clubs might be useful in many ways.

But the whole vexed question of moorings, such as their allocation and supervision etc., continued to engage the attention of members and committee alike for some time to come.

CHAPTER TWELVE

Enter the ladies

By the time this picture was taken, ladies were a natural inclusion in this annual dinner. In 1934, however, their presence was a novelty . . .

CLUB history was made at the annual dinner of 1934, held at the Sun Hotel, Chatham, when, for the very first time, ladies were present at what in the past, had always been an all-male occasion.

Commodore F. C. B. Baldwin told the ladies: "I hope it is coming up to your expectations and that you are enjoying yourselves as you think we probably did in years gone by." A sally that was greeted with the proverbial 'laughter'.

Two other points of interest emerged from this particular function. It was reported that the council had agreed to renew for seven years lease of the land on which the club operated at Rochester; and a very significant plea was advanced for inter-club racing, which was to follow some years later.

But back to those pre-war days of the 1930's. The club was still seeking a permanent foothold at Upnor and discussing the possible purchase of a section of the foreshore there.

Almost inevitably extra moorings were being sought and it was also decided to designate Upnor as a branch headquarters.

At about the same time young Mr. Weeks was seeking to interest members in establishing a fleet of Snipes, a class that was soon to feature in quite a big way at Rochester.

And support was being extended to the eventual formation of the Medway Yachting Association.

Snipes moored at the Rowing Club, Tower Reach, Rochester.

CHAPTER THIRTEEN

War clouds gather

This apparently idyllic sight reflects nothing of the gloom of impending war.

IN 1938 the words "crisis" and "emergency" were appearing in a national context in the minutes, but the club was still functioning normally in spite of the war clouds that were obviously gathering.

The social side of the club's activities was maintained with whist drives and dances, and it is interesting to note that it was agreed that dress for the annual dinner-dance of that year should be either evening or yachting. Apparently some members had not attended on previous occasions because of a dinner dress requirement!

Also in 1938 the club was delighted to receive an invitation to stage the 1939 National Snipe Championship races. A signal honour and distinction.

The offer was naturally accepted with alacrity and the club decided to order two boats to the latest Snipe specification to represent Medway in the championships.

Trophies and prize money were donated and the championships duly took place at Rochester from July 17th to 22nd, 1939. Racing was keen and Felix Gotto, of Standford Loch, Ulster, emerged as the winner in his boat, Happy Return.

When the Snipe championships were again held on the Medway, this time in 1949, they were sailed down river, at Upnor. Dr. W. C. Penman, of Northwich S.C. was the winner on this occasion, in Heatherpleat. Tom

Battleships brood over the Medway scene.

Snipe championships in full sail again, after the War.

Weekes, of Medway Y.C. was second in Kingfisher.

A little later, in September 1951 and July 1953, Medway again staged the Snipe national championships at Upnor. And the host club had the satisfaction of taking second place each time, firstly by Tom Weekes (again) and secondly through an up-and-coming young member, Nick Hodshon, who was to go on to gain sailing distinction at both national and international levels.

But back to May 1940, when Rear Commodore F. Parham presided over the 59th Annual General Meeting, "in the unavoidable absence on active service of Commodore F. Galbraith and Vice-Commodore F. Baldwin." There was a further emergency committee meeting on June 11th 1940, after which the club ceased to function until an informal meeting of members was called on Sunday, September 17th 1944.

The clubhouse would appear to have been used officially during the war by the National Fire Service and the local Home Guard and it was not until January 1946 that the premises again became freely available to the club.

'Girdler'. Auxiliary Gaff Cutter (N. Fortune-Fowler).

Aerial view of M.Y.C. boats, some at their moorings, others unde

'Huahine', West Solent Restricted Class.

T.S.M.Y. Forty-two (Norman West — Commodore 1948-49) comes to the aid of a capsized 18ft. National Dinghy, 'Amber'.

'Joya'. Auxiliary Cutter (H. Flory).

old training ship Arethusa before her departure to America.

'Kestrel'. Tom Weeke's Dragon, the first of the club's International Dragon Class.

'Ariel'. Auxiliary Cutter (M. Hamilton).

R. Clifford's 'Trinket'. (Owned today by C. I. Hagger and on the club listings after 29 years.)

'Thalassa'. Int. 6-metre (M. T. Knight, the tug owner).

Fireflies 'swarming' down the estuary.

Small dinghies like these mean anyone can enjoy 'messing about in boats'.

CHAPTER FOURTEEN

Back in business

WITHIN a matter of weeks the club was well and truly back in business. Several new members were elected, including ladies and cadets, and the club took part in a river display that featured in the local Victory Celebrations.

Mr. H. T. Callund, who had held the joint office of secretary-treasurer for 24 years, played a big part in getting things started again but announced that he could not continue to fill both roles. He recommended Mr. J. M., (Jack) Waights, as a possible new hon. secretary. Mr. Waights agreed to act and was duly elected, with Mr. Callund continuing as the hon. treasurer.

There is another treasurer today, but the hon. secretary, more than 30 years later, was still that same J. M. (Jack) Waights who, by that time was also a Trustee of the club he had served with such long and unbroken loyalty and devotion.

Jack Waites, honorary secretary for more than 30 years now.

Pop Parsons at the starting line.

At this stage it would also be appropriate to refer to another popular and long serving veteran, Mr. G. W. (Pop) Parsons, the club's hon. race officer.

A former R.A.F. man with a love of the sea, Pop once told an interviewer: "I've been here so long (since 1949) that the kids who were 20 when I first came are now turned 40 and bringing their children to see me."

That was a few years back but at the time of writing, Pop, like Jack, was still sailoring on.

Although they both probably won't thank this writer for saying it, there is not the slightest doubt that the Medway Yacht Club owes more than can be readily expressed in print to the likes of Jack Waights and Pop Parsons.

But back to those early post-second World War years.

CHAPTER FIFTEEN

Landing at Upnor

IN 1948 things were beginning to happen at Upnor. In June of that year the committee learned that a plot of ground fronting the foreshore at Upnor might soon become available on lease. It was decided to acquire it, providing the terms were right.

Hard on the heels of this important decision came a further piece of equally exciting news. It was reported that another plot of land could possibly be secured and it was naturally decided that further particulars of this should be sought.

In November it was reported that Mr. W. C. W. Brice had agreed to rent the club the first piece of land referred to above, but it had first to be de-requisitioned by the Admiralty.

In March of the following year, 1949, it was reported that the club was pressing on with the matter of acquiring Mr. Brice's land and estimates were being sought for necessary fencing and the reinstatement of an existing Nissen hut as a store.

June brought the more positive news that 200 feet of river frontage was being taken from Mr. Brice on a 99 years' lease "on extremely favourable terms", and further that 100 feet of river frontage to a depth of 900 feet was being purchased adjoining the leased site.

Things really were buzzing and a vote of thanks was accorded "to all those members instrumental in concluding a most satisfactory deal."

The additional piece of land it later transpired had been acquired from the A.P.C.M., the cement company, for, apparently, a sum of £180. That was 1949, of course. Just how much this sort of land would cost today is anybody's guess.

A few months later, in October, it was decided that plans for a new clubhouse at Upnor should be submit-

The old A.P.C.M. barge repair yard at Upnor, land now occupied by the Medway Yacht Club. The battleship Conqueror, seen right, was broken up in 1923.

ted to the local authority and that necessary applications should be made to the then Ministry of Town and Country Planning and to the licensing authorities.

There had always been a certain amount of uncertainty regarding the tenancy from the City Council of the club premises in Willis Avenue, Rochester, and this was reflected at the annual general meeting in January 1950. It was then proposed that in view of this uncertainty the club should proceed as soon as possible with the construction of a clubhouse at Upnor.

Up to then it had been club policy to provide all facilities at Upnor "but without a clubhouse". The decision of members was, however, that a clubhouse should be provided at Upnor "as soon as was convenient".

The die had been cast. The club was on its way down river.

In April 1950, the Ways and Means Committee reported that the minimum requirements for an Upnor clubhouse would cost £3,000. How should the club go about raising that sort of money? It could be done either by forming a limited company or by the issue of £10 debenture shares. it was decided to call an extraordinary general meeting to decide the matter.

This was duly held on June 9th when it was agreed that the necessary money should be raised among all members by the issue of £10 loan units. The target, remember, was £3,000, and members were assured that this was not excessive "bearing in mind present day costs." The word inflation had scarcely been heard of then!

One of Upnor's most distinctive features for many years — T. S. Arethusa.

A familiar site, but strangely empty, before development of the club premises.

CHAPTER SIXTEEN

A link is severed

Some of the club's early Dragons, seen racing on the Medway.

THE UPNOR project continued to progress and in almost no time at all a sum of £1,010 had been promised in loans. It was a total that quickly swelled.

Three months later a large Nissen hut had been purchased for £46, transported from Bekesbourne for an additional £11, and installed at Upnor by direct labour.

It was also decided to provide a second store hut, and further evidence, if it was needed, that the Medway Yacht Club was rapidly severing its links with Willis Avenue and Rochester Esplanade was demonstrated by the decision to hold the annual regatta buffet supper at Upnor, rather than at the Rochester clubhouse!

Things had certainly moved fast in the short space of just three months.

Another important decision, was taken in the summer of 1950, when it was decided to promote racing for Dragons, 12 feet national dinghies and Fireflies. The club was, in fact, to go on to build up one of the biggest Dragon fleets in the whole country.

But it was Upnor and the proposed new clubhouse that continued chiefly to concern both the committee and members in general. Various building plans and drafts were considered until, in January 1951, an estimate of £2,350 from a local builder was finally approved.

On Saturday, January 6th, 1951, Mrs. West, wife of former Commodore Norman West, was asked to turn the first spit.

The spade with which she performed the historic ceremonial act still occupies a special place in the clubhouse.

A dramatic view of the clubhouse by floodlight. The foundations were laid in 1951.

The building was naturally improved on and added to as the years went by and it is as well, perhaps, at this stage to reveal that the present imposing clubhouse nestling low on a hillside overlooking the river and the Dockyard and naval base on the opposite shore, boasts a luxurious lounge, dining room, galley, bars, changing rooms and showers.

There are also men's and women's bunk rooms, gear store, spar rack, workshop and library, plus, of course, car parks.

What more could anyone ask for, except, that is, a boat to sail in?

The old wooden structure at Rochester was, however, retained for a few more years after 1951, until complete administration was finally transferred to Upnor.

The physical link with Rochester above bridge had been finally severed.

Dragons proved to be a popular racing class, after the decision to promote them in the early 50's.

CHAPTER SEVENTEEN

Waltzing up the Medway

THE MEDWAY Club has always been noted for the generous hospitality readily extended to neighbouring clubs and, indeed, to visitors from more faraway places.

In the late summer of 1951, for instance, there sailed up the Medway to Upnor the 46 feet Bermuda cutter Waltzing Matilda which, as its name would suggest, hailed from Down Under. In reaching Upnor it had, in fact, ended a 16,000 mile voyage that had taken nearly a year to complete.

As was graphically reported at the time, "four hardy young Australians, one of them a woman, had proved conclusively to the world that the indomitable spirit of Frobisher and Drake is still alive."

The intrepid four comprised 33-year-old Sydney airlines pilot Philip Davenport, his attractive wife, Rosetta, his journalist brother, Keith, and Don Brown, a Queenslander.

They were said to have followed a route which had not been sailed since the old days of sailing ships, and which took them more than three-quarters of the way round the world.

But as one report of the time put it: "Adventure was nothing new to these three young men. They had all served as pilots in the Royal Australian Air Force in England during the war."

Rosetta, too, must have had quite an adventurous streak in her make-up!

At all events, the Australians were made honorary members of the yacht club during their stay at Upnor, and were accorded a special evening at which to meet and talk with members.

Philip Davenport, skipper of the Australian boat Waltzing Matilda, pictured (right) with club Commodore W. V. Price on a visit to the clubhouse.

A reference to their stay at Upnor was made in the book they wrote concerning their adventurous voyage, after returning to Australia. "Between times", wrote Philip Davenport, "we searched for a winter mooring until we found Upnor on the River Medway. Two days later Waltzing Matilda nosed her way into a soft mud berth on the outskirts of the tiny village. We have a gangplank to the shore and the tradesmen call at the door."

All 'mod. cons.' in fact!

A year or two later, in 1955, the American yawl Carina, winner of that year's Transatlantic Race from Newport, Rhode Island, U.S.A., to Marstrand, Sweden, and five races at Cowes, paid a visit to Upnor, where her owner and crew were entertained by the club.

The Stars and Stripes were an unusual but welcome sight on the Medway.

CHAPTER EIGHTEEN

The Cowes of Kent

Race Officer G. W. (Pop) Parsons proudly displays the new ensigns following the Royal Warrant permitting the club to "wear the Blue Ensigns of Her Majesty's Fleet," granted in 1953.

THE ANNUAL regattas staged by the Medway club grew in both size and popularity and the record entries attracted by the 1953 event prompted one enthusiastic visitor to describe Upnor as "The Cowes of Kent".

In this particular year, for the first time, the regatta extended into a third day. The daily entries numbered 150 and at one time, it was said, something like 700 people were afloat.

The year 1953 was, in fact, a notable one in the history of the club, for it was then that it received the Admiralty Warrant. This is an important distinction that permits the club and its member yachts "to wear the Blue Ensign of Her Majesty's Fleet".

Very few clubs other than Royal yacht clubs can claim this distinction. How fitting and deserved it would be if that honour should, perhaps, come as the club enters into its second century of existence!

But as someone, somewhere, sagely observed, we must wait and see. At the time of writing, at least.

The following year the club was again very much in the news when its summer ball was held in most nautical surroundings — aboard the Training Ship Arethusa, which for many years was a familiar sight at her Upnor moorings, not far from the

National 18's in full sail at the 1953 regatta.

Medway Club's present headquarters.

One of the last windjammers still afloat, the Arethusa (formerly Peking), was a training ship for boys destined to go on to join either the Royal or Merchant Navies. She was specially illuminated (lit up!) for the ball, with the after-deck as a dance floor, and music by a Royal Marines band.

It was, as can be imagined, a gay and colourful occasion and one that was to be repeated. But like so many other of England's historic treasures, Arethusa became too expensive to maintain and some years later she was sold to the South Street Seaport Museum of New York, America.

Her new owners restored her original name, Peking, and also her original rig as a four-masted barque. As Peking, they said at the time "she is still earning her living here, letting people learn about the stern and relentless life of an ocean-going merchant ship."

But New York's gain, was undoubtedly Medway's loss. Upnor doesn't seem quite the same without the Arethusa.

A sad sight as the T. S. Arethusa sets out from Upnor for her new home in New York harbour. The date: March 7th, 1975.

T. S. Arethusa, specially decorated with lights for the M.Y.C. ball.

Members and guests at the summer ball held aboard the old Training Ship Arethusa.

Rear-Commodore (Mr. H. Dyer), Commodore (Mr. M. Hamilton), Vice-Commodore (Mr. J. Field) and their wives aboard the Arethusa.

CHAPTER NINETEEN

A royal regatta

THE YEAR 1957 brought further distinction to the club. Rear Commodore David Clarabut (later to become Commodore), his wife Deirdre (a keen yachtswoman) and Dr. A. Travers Rogers, took part with the Duke of Edinburgh in a special Royal Regatta at Copenhagen, during Her Majesty the Queen's visit to Denmark.

The regatta was organised by the Danish Dragon Club to commemorate the Queen's visit, and Mr. Clarabut's dragon-class boat Snapdragon, was transported to Copenhagen on board the Royal yacht Britannia, together with the Duke's own Bluebottle. Mr. and Mrs. Clarabut and Dr. Rogers made their own way by rail and sea.

The invitation to take part in this Royal event was rightly looked upon as quite an honour, not only for the three participants but also for the Medway club itself.

Two years earlier Bluebottle had taken part in a special series of races at Upnor, arranged by the M.Y.C., and this fact could have had some bearing on the Royal invitation to Copenhagen that was to follow.

Bluebottle had been presented to the Queen and Prince Philip as a wedding present and her arrival on the Medway naturally aroused tremendous local interest. Her sailing master at the time was Lt. Cdr. Graham Mann and she finished fourth in her first race, as part of a Royal Norfolk and Suffolk Y.C. team.

The next day Bluebottle was sailed by Tom Weekes in the Medway Y.C. team and Tom brought her in first.

Bluebottle, the Duke's boat, and her racing flag. A place of honour on the clubhouse wall.

Bluebottle's racing flag was subsequently presented to the Medway Club and, suitably framed and inscribed, it now occupies a place of honour on the clubhouse wall.

CHAPTER TWENTY

Wet seat and flowing sail

Harold Dyer's 'Escape'.

H. A. Dyer, Commodore (1957 & 58), presented the club with Drake's Drum for cruisers.

Firefly class, contenders for the Pants and Bailer trophy.

THIS book would not be complete without reference to some, at least, of the many club trophies.

Pride of place, but not necessarily in terms of importance, must surely go to the quaintly named Pants and Bailer trophy. This came into being in 1952, when it was presented to the club by the Firefly class.

It was laid down that it was to be "competed for annually at the club premises at Upnor between teams of Fireflies composed of three boats to each team representing a club recognised by the Yachting Association and racing in accordance with the rules of the class." Phew!

Invitations to compete, it was further decreed, should be issued by the Medway Club. The intriguing title is probably suggestive of a "wet seat and a flowing sail", and it is certainly one to catch the eye as well as the imagination of all yachtsmen.

Fireflies 'in the scrum' below the clubhouse.

A club trophy with a much more romantic sound to it is Drake's Drum, for cruisers. This trophy, presented by former Commodore H. A. Dyor, naturally serves as a reminder of the local link with the great Sir Francis Drake, and the legend of his ship's drum.

Another well-known trophy is the Medway Bowl, donated by the club in 1949, as a perpetual challenge trophy for the southern section of the Y.R.A. national 18 feet class championships, competed for under the auspices of the M.Y.C. There are also numerous other trophies to be won by members.

In 1959, the ladies really came into their own, when it was decided that "the ladies race to take place on Sunday, July 19th, can be competed for in dinghies up to and including the national 18 feet class." Mrs. Wyllie would certainly have approved of this!

National 18's compete for the Medway Bowl.

CHAPTER TWENTY-ONE

Medway Week is born

M.Y.C. clubhouse, headquarters for the Medway Yachting Week.

PREVIOUS references have been made to the old Medway Yachting Association which ceased to function at the outbreak of the Second World War, and which did not make its expected early revival.

The small sum of money held in the Association's banking account was, in fact, handed over to the Medway Club who decided to use it for the provision of a trophy for competition among clubs previously affiliated to the Association. That was in 1955.

Three years later, in June 1958, Medway Yachting Week was born. The Medway club was joined by the Royal Engineers Y.C., the Royal Naval Sailing Association, Medway Cruising Club and Sheppey Y.C., in staging a week's programme of racing that attracted entries from all parts of the country.

The Medway had long been regarded as one of the premier yachting centres in England and it was felt that there was a big need for such an event on the river.

It was at this first Medway Week that the Drake's Drum trophy was put up for competition for the first time. Somewhat ironically it was won by — a soldier, Brigadier G. W. Duke, of the local Royal Engineers!

The Y.M.C. clubhouse at Upnor was an obvious choice as headquarters for the Week, which was voted a huge success, from both the racing and social points of view. It was, in fact, the biggest regatta ever held on the Medway.

Dragons picking up speed.

A helping hand from the ladies, as boats are made ready for sailing.

Making ready to set out.

CHAPTER TWENTY-TWO

Return of the Dutch

THE 1960's saw the club firmly established at Upnor in every possible way. Racing was being sponsored for several classes including Hornets, Flying 15's, Swordfish, Dragons, Snipes and 5-0-5's. There was handicap racing for sailing cruisers and dinghies, and a small motorboat section was also in existence.

People were almost clamouring to join the club and it was very much a case of taking your place in the queue to obtain membership which, as from the very start, was by nomination and election. Some restriction had of necessity to be placed on the total membership and then, as now, there was a waiting list for full membership.

Late in 1962 the cruiser committee reported that they "had boats in the Mediterranean, the Baltic and almost everywhere between the north of Spain and Denmark." At one stage, it was said, there were 16 of the club yachts in Holland at the same time.

Five of them met at Muiden in the Zuider Zee, to take part in a race of the Royal Netherlands Yacht Squadron. Handed over to the Dutch Squadron was the de Ruyter Cannon Ball International Trophy, a Dutch shot fired against Upnor Castle in 1667, made into a trophy, and presented by a group of Medway yachtsmen.

This interesting item permits the jump in time we now make to June, 1967, when, as mentioned, in the introduction to this book, the Dutch made another foray up the Medway, to Gillingham and Upnor. This time they came in friendship.

Rear-Commodore F. R. Crossley, instrumental in organising the Medway Dutch Week. (Mr. Crossley was Commodore in 1971 and '72.)

The occasion was Medway Dutch Week, for which there was a big programme of events, including, of course, a Medway Dutch Week Regatta. It was sponsored by British Petroleum Co. Ltd. the largest firm using the river, and was organised by a committee drawn from all the main yacht clubs on the river.

More than 60 Dutch boats came over for the week's racing, which was controlled by a sailing committee under Capt. Eric Johnson, R.N., with the general administration being car-

Definitely no sailing on this day! The winter of '62-'63 will be remembered by many, when ice covered the Medway.

ried out by a committee headed by Rear Commodore F. R. Crossley, of the Medway Yacht Club.

The Dutch yachtsmen had their fair share of success in the week's racing and Medway also figured among the prize-winners. It is interesting to note that the Royal Netherlands Y.C. boat Bem won the Royal Naval Sailing Association trophy — "to be competed for next in AD 2067"!

Needless to say, the Medway Y.C. was also well to the fore in the social aspects of what, in every way, was a memorable "return anniversary visit" by the men from Holland.

Four months later, in November, Queen Juliana of the Netherlands honoured three local men for the parts they had played in organising Medway Dutch Week.

One of them was Brigadier B. Chichester-Cooke, of the Medway Club, who was invested as an officer of the Order of Oranje-Nassau, for his help in organising the yachting events. Also honoured were Councillor Ron Foster and Town Clerk Roy Hill, of Chatham, chairman and secretary respectively of the Week Committee.

CHAPTER TWENTY-THREE

A battle of words

IN THE mid-1960's, the club was one of many similar interested parties engaged in what might be termed a running battle of words with the Central Electricity Generating Board.

The Board was proposing to build a jetty in Long Reach, near Hoo, to serve their Kingsnorth generating station. The Medway club expressed great concern regarding the jetty's close proximity to the Darnett Ness, where it was said, "the fairway is narrow and takes a sharp bend which would create an unnecessary hazard, particularly when vessels were rounding up to berth."

The Generating Board stressed what it considered to be the national importance of the generating station, but said it was prepared to incorporate reasonable measures for the protection of small craft.

The view of the yachting and sailing clubs associated with the Medway was that the jetty scheme would seriously restrict racing on the river "and the free use and enjoyment of a large area of sailing water."

Meetings between the Generating Board and the various river clubs concerned in the matter were held at R.Y.A. headquarters in London. At this time the Medway club was talking in terms of asking the Board to consider paying for the total cost of moving the Yacht Club "to a point somewhere below the jetty."

Some Board members are said to have agreed that the cost of this would be low in comparison with any modification to their plans, and they did not rule it out as a possibility! As we know, there was no such move, but the arguments concerning the jetty continued unabated.

A trial race was even arranged by the Queen's Harbour Master, Chatham, over a course simulated to include the proposed jetty. This took place and apparently convinced the Board that there could be a hazard as well as an inconvenience to craft on the river.

But some yachtsmen were reported to have been surprised at the amount of river which remained available and felt that "all would become accustomed to it."

The Board, however, agreed to shorten the jetty "as much as possible" and to one or two other minor modifications, and there the matter eventually ended, or rather continued in the hands of the Generating Board, the Medway Conservancy Board and the Admiralty. In other words, it was — carry on sailing as usual!

CHAPTER TWENTY-FOUR

Ashore and afloat

A typical waterfront scene, with a small but determined canine guard on the untended boat in the left foreground.

IN THE summer of 1964 the club provided facilities for Oxford v. Cambridge sailing match, and loaned some of their Flying 15's to the competing Varsity crews. For the record, Oxford won the match 4-1.

A training scheme for cadet members was started at about this time, under the direction of Mr. R. Ballantyne. It was voted a great success, with as many as 30 cadets under instruction.

In August of this year the Hoad brothers, Tim and Bill, finished 4th overall in the 5-0-5 world championships, sailed in Cork Harbour. They had previously finished second in the national championships at Plymouth, in their boat Eruption.

The 1964 minute book also recorded a most thirst provoking item. The brewers, it seemed, had anounced a halfpence a pint increase in the price of bitter beer. It was, however,

The 1965 Medway Regatta was the biggest ever, but Upnor's facilities had reached saturation point.

agreed that there should be no increase in the price at the bar, (1/7d), "as the club still made 5d. a pint profit."

Enough, surely, to make today's beer drinkers shed tears into their astronomically priced pints!

There was plenty of activity both afloat and ashore as the club moved confidently towards the 1970s. The 1965 Medway Regatta was the biggest ever, with entries up by more than 100.

It was, in fact, getting a little too big for comfort as far as the Medway Club was concerned, and whose Upnor facilities were said to have reached saturation point at regatta time.

It was later suggested that the club should revert to holding its own individual regatta. Instead, it was decided to ask the Medway Regatta Committee to continue organising the event on similar lines as before, "but restricting entries and scope to more reasonable proportions, bearing in mind the general facilities available."

Plans were also afoot to form an association of Medway Yacht Clubs and the outcome was that the regatta committee was eventually reconstituted as the Medway Yachting Association as we know it today. Its aims were:- (1) To watch over all matters that are of common interest to yachtsmen using the Medway and Swale, and (2) Annually conduct the Medway Regatta.

The club chalked up a notable success in 1966 when David Cole, in Brigand Chief, went over to Holland and won the Flevo Cup, a trophy never previously won by anyone other than a Dutchman. And M. Whitecross, in Poseidon, was second overall in the Hornet world championships at Zegrze in Poland.

In 1967, the Medway club spoke out in no uncertain voice in support of the Kent County Council. Both took the view "that the southern area of the Medway should be retained for its scientific interest, or improved to give greater public access for leisure purposes."

This, it appeared, was directly contrary to the views of the Medway Conservancy Board who, it was claimed, "look upon the development of practically the whole of the river as a modern international port."

Medway Y.C. were prepared to provide evidence as to the need to "preserve, promote and extend facilities for yachting on the River Medway."

The outcome of all this was the formation of the River Medway Amenities Preservation Society, in which Rear Commodore Dr. S. J. Cox played a leading part.

CHAPTER TWENTY-FIVE

Loyal service rewarded

PREVIOUS reference has been made to the outstanding service accorded to the club by Hon. Secretary Jack Waights, and Hon. Race Officer Pop Parsons.

It will come as no surprise, therefore, to learn that suitable recognition was to be accorded to both of these stalwarts. In 1967, members donated what was to be known as the Pop Parsons Trophy in appreciation of the race officer's work on their behalf.

The trophy, it was decided, should be competed for annually and awarded to the helmsman of the first boat home sailed by a junior or cadet member in the club's Medway marathon event.

A year later, in March 1968, the club showed its appreciation of Mr. Waights' 21 years' dedicated service. It took the form of a presentation wrist watch and two paintings of the club. There was also a gift for Mrs. Waights, who had also served the club well in a variety of ways and, like her husband, still does.

Both Mr. and Mrs. Waights were further honoured by being elected life members.

Two years later, in December 1970, there was further recognition for Pop Parsons, who then had also completed 21 years' service. He received a wrist watch and a cheque, the Commodore (Dr. A. T. Rogers) observing that Pop's Line was "the envy of all the clubs in the south east."

That the club was continuing its programme of expansion is revealed in the decision taken at this time to purchase a further piece of land at Upnor and also to acquire the freehold of the land currently held on lease from Mr. Brice.

A revolutionary step on the domestic front, was the appointment of what was to be termed a club manager. The new man was put in charge of bar, catering and cleaning staffs, but was still, of course, responsible overall to the Hon. Secretary.

It worked well enough for a time but the club eventually reverted to the well-tried formula of steward and stewardess with the necessary ancillary staff, a system still operating today.

Hon. Race Officer Pop Parsons.

Long-serving Hon. Secretary J. M. (Jack) Waights.

CHAPTER TWENTY-SIX

An upward look

HAVING accomplished the successful move down river to Upnor, the year 1969 saw the club casting its eyes in another direction — upwards this time. The need was coming, it was felt, to provide a second storey to the clubhouse.

It was obviously not an immediate possibility but the general feeling was that it should be placed high on the list of the club's future financial priorities. And there it still remains today, but with every chance of becoming reality fairly early on in the M.Y.C.'s second century of existence.

It will, however, cost a great deal more than the £10,000 that was estimated in 1969.

There was good news for the club's veteran members at this time. It was agreed that those of them who had reached the age of 65 and who had held continuous membership for a minimum of 10 years should pay only half the normal membership fee. A nice gesture.

At the other end of the age scale, Medway's Nicholas Martin, was a crew member of the winning boat in the Enterprise Junior World Championships sailed in Hamilton, Bermuda.

Also in 1969, race officer Pop Parsons was reporting that it had been an excellent season for the Wayfarers, a popular all-purpose type boat. "Since their adoption as a class they have proved a great asset to the club," Pop reported.

That he was not exaggerating is shown by the fact that the Wayfarers were to build up to the biggest fleet in the club, at one time topping 60.

The Flying 15's were also well to the fore at this time, setting a then club record of more than 500 starters in a season. The Southern Area championships for the class were held at Upnor and voted a great success.

As usual, Pop paid tribute to his "wonderful team of ladies" who, week after week, gave up their time to run the line. And, again as usual, Pop 'said it with flowers' to his ladies at the end of the season. Among those named as helpers in the starter's box were Margaret Townshend; Gill Wilson; Joy Gray; Mollie Shephard; Joan Greenfield; Doris Hodshon and Joan Wright.

A couple of years later Pop was in different mood, directing a blast at some at least of the male members for what he described as a sad deterioration in sailing discipline.

He was referring specifically to retirements, signing on, launching, and the safety boat. Organisation of the latter he said, did not work with its usual efficiency, "mostly because Skippers did not turn up".

Pop's criticisms were passed on to the class captains, hopefully with the desired effect.

Southern Area championships for the Flying 15's were held at Upnor in 1969.

CHAPTER TWENTY-SEVEN

A worrying time

THE YEAR 1971 opened on a cautionary note, with the treasurer reporting that money was being spent at an alarming rate. The bar was said to be doing well but the catering department, as on some previous occasions, was not satisfactory from a financial point of view. All the various committees were asked to study their budgets for the months ahead.

It would be fair to say, however, that eventually the position on the catering front was to be put on a much sounder footing in terms of profit and loss. The quality of the food served had never been in question.

An even bigger cloud was, however, hanging over the club at this particular stage of its history. The then Strood Rural District Council (later to be replaced by the more powerful Medway Council), was reported to have been given planning permission for the development of Upnor Village.

Mr. Stuart Campkin, a previous Club Steward, overlooking his domain.

And the council's plans were said to include the possible compulsory purchase of the Yacht Club's existing car and trolley park, leaving them with only a small triangular part of the land at their disposal.

The land was held on lease from the A.P.C.M., and the yachtsmen made an immediate offer of £10,000 to the Cement Company for its outright acquisition.

To no avail, Strood Council, it was revealed, were poised to secure the land on behalf of a firm of developers, whose cash offer was obviously going to be more acceptable to the A.P.C.M. than that made by the yacht club.

There was, however, still the chance that the yachtsmen would be offered some part of the land. But nothing was certain and it was a difficult and worrying time for the yachting fraternity, especially as it was thought that some of their moorings could be lost to them as a result of the proposed development.

The land was eventually acquired by the developers concerned, but assurances were forthcoming that the interests of the yacht club "would be borne in mind."

A further complication was to arise in 1973, when it was learned that the land had been resold to yet another firm of developers and, as far as the yacht club was concerned, negotiations would have to commence all over again from the original starting point.

In June 1973, the new developers were said to be considering the club's offer to buy the land but the negotiations were described as being both

It was not until 1977 that the land originally owned by A.P.C.M. was eventually acquired by the yacht club.

difficult and protracted. A little later, however, in the following December, it was said that a decision could be expected "any minute now."

As things turned out that "minute" was to stretch into weeks, months and even years. By 1974 the Strood Rural District Council had been superseded by the new Medway Council, whose chief executive, Mr Roy Hill, was promising in August of that year to expedite the matter of the proposed land deal as far as the yacht club was concerned.

A site discussion was arranged for the following month and, thankfully, from the yacht club's point of view, the Sports Council said that its earlier promise of a grant towards the purchase price would remain open, in spite of the long delay that was being experienced.

In November, Medway Council said the matter had been passed to its Planning and Legal Department. At the club's A.G.M. Commodore R. P. Townshend referred to what he described as the interminable negotiations that had gone on for years, "and had not been possible to resolve."

And so it went on, with the yacht club caught up between the local council and the developers, in discussions that continued to ebb and flow without seemingly getting anywhere.

All things must, however, come to an end at some time and so, eventually in 1977, the yacht club finally secured title to the land they had so assiduously sought to acquire. But it was to cost them £30,000, three times the amount originally estimated.

It did mean, however, that Medway Yacht Club was to become the proud and unchallenged owners of all that land at Upnor on which its many shore based activities are carried out.

Commodore R. P. Townshend, caught up in the interminable negotiations of land deals.

CHAPTER TWENTY-EIGHT

The little ships

Not long after Nick Hodshon had won back the Pants and Bailer trophy in a Wayfarer, Mr. W. G. S. Hodshon died, and the Bill Hodshon Trophy was provided for the Wayfarer class.

OTHER things were, of course, happening within the club during the time that so much attention had centred on the A.P.C.M. land question, so fully dealt with in the preceding chapter.

Memories of the dark days of Dunkirk were revived on May 31st, 1971, when the R.Y.A. Little Ships Anniversary rally was held at Upnor. Many boats and personalities took part, including B.B.C. celebrity Raymond Baxter.

Facilities and entertainment for the crews of the little ships were provided at the clubhouse, and many letters of appreciation of the hospitality extended were subsequently addressed to the club.

Other visitors to Upnor at about this time included three Australian boats, Salacia II, Ragamuffin and Koomooloo, which had come over for the Admiral's Cup race. Moorings were provided for them from the middle of June to the beginning of July, and a dinner for the crews was held at the club.

The summer of this year saw D. Townshend win the National Swordfish Championship at Poole, sailing in Heron, with R. Brodie.

Another success on the sailing front was achieved by the club's A team of N. Hodshon, A. Wilson and K. Grinter, who won the Pants and Bailer Trophy against visiting teams from Wembley and Laleham, the first time in five years that Medway had won this, their own trophy.

An even bigger distinction came Nick Hodshon's way a week or two later when he won the Wayfarers' National title at Hayling, in Nipegegi.

On a more domestic note, 1971 saw the decision taken to introduce central heating to the club, a move that was later said to have added considerably to the comfort of members.

A sadder note was struck by the death of long-serving member Mr. W. G. S. Hodshon. A memorial fund was started and resulted in the later provision of the Bill Hodshon Trophy for competition in the Wayfarer class.

That well-known Atlantic rower, Chay Blyth was a visitor in 1972, when a lecture he had agreed to give attracted so much interest that it had to be switched to the greater seating capacity afforded by the gymnasium at the Chatham Naval Base.

Another earlier distinguished visitor to the Medway Club had been round-the-world yachtsman Sir Alec Rose.

This year, too, saw the introduction of a sartorial note in the club's affairs. There had been some discussion as to the standard of dress to be worn in the clubhouse, particularly at night.

The House Committee gave the matter their considered opinion and recommended that no rigid rules should be imposed. Members, they said, should, however, be encouraged to maintain a reasonable standard, including casual clothes.

The committee further suggested that a wide standard should be accepted, provided they met with normal social obligations as applicable to a yacht club.

In July, a party of 20 juniors from the North Sea Y.C. came over from Ostend and were entertained to a week-long programme of racing and social events.

Koomooloo, one of the three yachts moored at Upnor in preparation for the Admiral's Cup race.

It was, of course, Olympics year and Nick Hodshon, with crewmen Robert Cox and Mike James, took part in the national trials in Nick's Soling boat, Searcher III, and, according to reports, came very near to Olympic selection. "A fine effort indeed," observed Commodore F. R. Crossley.

In April, 1973, the Sailing Committee reported that the first fibreglass Dragon had arrived at the club. It was the Pegasus, owned by K. Best.

CHAPTER TWENTY-NINE

Voice of protest

A typical Upnor scene, showing club moorings and the distinctive dolphins.

IN MAY, 1973, the Sailing Committee raised its voice in protest over the increase in power boat racing on the river. The matter was subsequently referred to the Medway Yachting Association, with the satisfactory result to the men of sail that power boat racing was limited to four times a year.

A year later, early in 1974, the club was clearly conscious of its approaching centenary, and a subcommittee was set up to consider what should be done to mark the important occasion.

The 1974 Medway Regatta proved to be an event that elicited both praise and a certain amount of criticism. The M.Y.C. Sailing Committee considered it to have been a good event, with entries up by 25 per cent, but had reservations on one or two points.

What it all boiled down to was that the Medway clubmen considered that sponsorship of the event should be sought and parking and mooring facilities improved so that invitations could be extended to south and east coast clubs, plus those from Holland, Belgium and Denmark.

These important suggestions were

passed on to the Medway Yachting Association. A year later it was reported that Vice-Commodore P. N. Harvey had written to the Regatta chairman regarding "the concern felt on the possible number of entries expected for dinghies, cruisers, etc. in view of the extensive publicity and the international aspect of the 1975 Regatta and the danger of overloading the facilities of the M.Y.C."

It was the old, old story, of course, and other clubs were again asked to say what accommodation they could provide during the Regatta, to ease the burden invariably placed on Medway.

In September 1974, Mr. Bob Bullen was appointed the club's full-time Bosun, and was quick to earn widespread commendation for the manner in which he went about his duties.

The club now also has its own professional Coxswain in Mr. Len Cowen, and it should be recorded that there are two safety boats, the Kent and the Bellis, a trot boat (Invicta), and two mooring barges, Roper and Roffen.

On-shore facilities for the benefit of members include electrically operated winches, gantries, derricks, tractors, and outside power point boxes at strategic spots. Fresh water is laid on to the outer of the club's two dolphins. Almost nothing, it seems, has been overlooked for the all-round use and benefit of members.

But back to 1974 and the bombshell that was then dropped from the starter's box at the end of the sailing season. In his report, race officer Pop Parsons, who, owing to an accident to his wife, had been unable to carry out his duties from the middle of August, suggested that the time had come for him to relinquish a post he had filled and enjoyed for 25 years.

"I shall be 78 next June," said Pop, but added that he was still prepared to help out in a number of ways. The thought of a starter's box without Pop Parsons in it to supervise his team of ladies was almost unthinkable, and in January 1975, the Sailing Committee was able to report (sighs of relief) that Pop had agreed to sailor-on. But not, perhaps, every weekend.

So arrangements had to be made for deputy race officers, and attention was given to the training and briefing of Officers of the Day, "in order to ensure the efficient running of the Line when Mr. Parsons is not on duty."

All, or nearly all, was well again on the Line.

The very success of the 1974 Medway Regatta caused some criticism, because of the overloading of facilities at M.Y.C. Parking and mooring was a matter for concern, with entries up by 25 per cent.

CHAPTER THIRTY

A dry round

THE YEAR 1975 had opened on what can only be described as a dry note. Owing to an unfortunate oversight the club's registration with the licensing magistrates was not renewed. This meant that drinks could not be served on the premises.

There was no alternative but to close the bars and return to the brewers such draught beer as was in stock but could not be sold.

A month was, in fact, to go by before it was possible to make the necessary application for renewal of the club's registration, and when this had been successfully accomplished, a relieved and grateful House Committee expressed thanks to the Hon. Secretary "for having attended court on behalf of the club."

It is not difficult to imagine what must have been the agonising frustration of members during those weeks when the M.Y.C. was, quite literally, the club with no beer!

There was happy news from the Sailing Committee. They reported that Mr. T. Kirby had been elected chairman of the National Wayfarers' Association. On an even broader sailing front the decision was taken for the Medway club to become fully affiliated to the R.Y.A.

A suggestion that some of the land on the former Cockham Slipway — earlier acquired by the club — should be utilised as a caravan or camping site was not favourably received. It was considered that the provision of toilet and other facilities for this would be too expensive.

1975 saw the introduction of cadet racing in the Mirror dinghies.

Instead, it was felt that the slipway would, without undue expense, provide an amenity for members in cases of repairs that necessitated hauling out.

February 1975, saw the appointment of Mr. T. D. Gurney as club hon. treasurer. A chartered accountant, Mr. Gurney had previously held office as chairman of the Entertainments Committee.

In his new role of treasurer, he made a comprehensive study of the club's finances and advanced recommendations that involved various economies and an overall increase of 25 per cent in membership fees and other club charges.

These measures were subsequently approved, but not, of course, without discussion and some small measure of opposition, as was only to be expected. They were, however, designed to put the club on a sound financial course.

This year also saw permission given to implement racing for cadet members, and this was later described by the race officer as one of the best things introduced by the club. "These youngsters really enjoy the chance to race," Pop Parsons declared.

The cadets did their racing in Mirror dinghies with, of course, all necessary precautions as to safety and supervision.

Some notable sailing successes were also achieved by the club's senior members. A. J. Wilson won the 1975 National Wayfarers' championship at Plymouth, with P. Warner placed 3rd, and G. Hodshon 4th. Warner had previously won the Southern Area championship at Poole, and on that occasion Wilson had to be content with 3rd place.

In the Hornet European championships at the Thorpe Bay Club, Medway Y.C. boats were placed 6th, 15th, 16th and 18th out of 78 entries, the best club result of any fleet taking part.

Back home at Upnor, however, concern was being expressed at the decline in Hornet racing on the Medway. Theoretically, Medway had the biggest Hornet fleet in the country and it was agreed that the class captain had done everything to encourage more sailing.

A Firefly open meeting on two days in August was said to have taken place "in incredibly good weather — blazing sunshine and force 4 winds". Six teams competed for the Pants and Bailer trophy, which was won by Laleham S.C.

At the club's annual meeting Miss S. Sobernheim raised the question of lady membership, "in view of impending legislation."

Concern was expressed at the lack of Hornet racing even though Medway had the biggest fleet of that class.

She was told that the committee would give the matter consideration as soon as the full implications of the new law on Sex Discrimination were known.

Suffice it here to say that the club still has what is known as lady members, but many members of the fair sex are also full members and active sailors. Including Miss Sobernheim, who became captain of the club's Firefly class.

Readers will recall that the club had a much earlier feminine hand on the tiller. That of Mrs. Wyllie, in Maid of Kent and other boats. Which shows that there is no discrimination when it comes to sailing, as several other ladies have so demonstrably proved.

CHAPTER THIRTY-ONE

Fluctuating fortunes

THE YEAR 1976 opened on a highly promising note with no fewer than 75 new members, plus two cadets, being elected to the club. But it was not a case of roses all the way. Later in the year it was revealed that the club had experienced an overall loss of almost £700.

The House Committee met the loss that had occurred in their department by slapping on modest increases in the price of tea and coffee and adding two pence to all drinks over the bar.

On a wider financial front, the treasurer asked for, and eventually got, a 15 per cent increase in subscriptions and other charges. Members were told that any attempted economies would mean a serious lowering of the standards they then enjoyed.

The club's need for the extra income was not far to seek. The 1977 maintenance budget alone was an estimated £5,500, including one item of £1,500 for a general electrical overhaul and rewiring of the clubhouse.

Consternation at the club house grew over losses on the financial side, and money had to be raised by increased charges all round.

At this time, too, of course, the club was concerned with finding the cash needed for the A.P.C.M. land deal then shortly to be finalised, and dealt with at length in a previous chapter.

In addition to the subscription and other increases that were agreed to, it was also decided to raise additional funds by means of interest free £10 debenture shares, a method that had been employed, it will be remembered, to finance the Upnor clubhouse.

It was further agreed to the election of a maximum of 40 Life Members. Those eligible for this status, it was decided, must be over 50 and to have been full members for at least 10 consecutive years. They would be required to pay a fee 10 times that of full membership. The General Committee were also empowered to borrow, if necessary.

As we know, the deal did go through and, all things being equal, everything seemed set fair for the club from now on.

It did not mean that the time would not again come when extra income might have to be raised. Inflation, and that second storey dream, could well mean further financial demands in the future.

Other things were also happening during the course of the year. Three members took part in the Wayfarer World Championships in Toronto, the club making a contribution towards

Southern championships at Upnor for Flying 15s were held in August, 1976.

their expenses. The trio did quite well too, A. J. Wilson finishing 12th, P. R. Warner 13th, and P. Strauss 15th.

Wilson had earlier won the Southern, and (at Upnor), the Eastern championships in this class, but the national title had gone to another M.Y.C. member, G. Hodshon. Wilson was placed 3rd on this occasion.

The Flying 15's Southern championships were sailed at Upnor in August, but the highest placing Medway could manage was 4th by E. Shephard.

That hardy annual the Medway Regatta was also up for discussion once again. Various unspecified alternatives are said to have been considered, but Vice-Commodore P. N. Harvey revealed that it was the unanimous view of the club's Sailing Committee that the regatta should continue in its present form.

Further support for this point of view seemed to come from Commodore Dr. S. J. Cox, who felt that as the senior club on the river, the Medway Y.C. had a responsibility when it came to providing facilities for a regatta. And that seemed to be very much that, as far as the club and the Medway Regatta were concerned.

There was a further sartorial reminder in the summer of 1976. The House Committee agreed that it should be proclaimed on the notice board that members were requested to observe reasonable standards, "it being considered that bathing costumes, lack of shirts or footwear are not considered acceptable in the clubhouse."

The Sailing Committee this year recommended that the Lasers, which had chalked up 159 starts, should be adopted as a sponsored class, with races on Saturdays and Sundays.

Mr. T. R. Kirby was congratulated on his work in re-writing the club's sailing instructions in what was described as logical order. He had also, it was reported, put forward suggestions for new courses together with a proposal that the river should be divided into three areas, each of 17 courses.

Thanks also went to Mr. Rex May for all the work he had put in driving the club tractor, together with good wishes for his new career in the Navy. And Race Officer Pop Parsons congratulated Chris Ries on the excellent job he had done in organising the safety boats.

Wayfarers fared well in Toronto, as well as at home in the Southern and Eastern championships.

The distinctive single-handed Lasers were coming into their own in 1976, when they were first adopted by the club as a sponsored class.

Some concern was expressed among sailing clubs at this time over a proposal to introduce a regular hovercraft service from Strood Pier to Sheerness and Southend. Trials were said to have taken place when there was no racing in progress, but doubt seems to have existed as to whether such a service would be a commercial proposition.

Whatever the reason, hovercrafts have not so far invaded the Medway in the local area suggested.

Two years later, however, the alarm bells started ringing again. It was not hovercraft this time, but hydrofoils.

Towards the end of 1978 a retired naval officer revealed that he was considering the possibilities of establishing a high speed river link between Chatham, Sheerness, Southend and London.

The vessels he was proposing to bring into service for this ambitious venture were 71-seater Sunrise hydrofoils, built in Russia and said to be capable of speeds exceeding 30 knots.

The very thought of these sort of vessels speeding up and down the Medway on a regular schedule was, of course, disturbing to say the least as far as yachtsmen were concerned. The M.Y.C., together with other clubs on the river, naturally geared themselves to maintain a careful watch on the survey which it was said was being carried out on the hydrofoil proposal.

The year 1976 had brought a nostalgic item of news when Vice-Commodore Harvey reported that he had seen and photographed the former T. S. Arethusa in New York harbour, "where she looked extremely well kept and fully rigged."

The "Old Girl," it seemed, was in good hands.

CHAPTER THIRTY-TWO

The last echoes

'An ever increasing asset' — the club's land was made finally secure by completion of the A.P.C.M. deal.

IT WILL have been obvious to readers that this history of the club has been compiled on more or less chronological lines. So it must here be recorded that the last echoes of the vital former A.P.C.M. land deal were sounded early in 1977.

The deal was, in fact, finally completed on February 14th, 1977, after protracted negotiations spanning something like 8 years. Patience had been ultimately rewarded.

In the words of past Commodore Stuart Cox the club now owned "all the land it requires on the best stretch of river and have an ever increasing asset to take with it into its second century."

Not that the club was content to sit back happy in the knowledge that its tenure at Upnor was fully secure. The Site and Works Committee was soon busy preparing a report that envisaged improvements in several directions.

Among the priorities listed was an extension to the clubhouse, hard standing for cruisers, improvements to the sea wall and the boat and car parks, together with the re-routing of power and telephone cables, among other things. The total cost of all the work involved was estimated at £20,000 plus.

In the background, too, was the long cherished dream of a second storey to the clubhouse.

It was, of course, the Royal Jubilee year and a special and very successful Jubilee race for cruisers was held by the club on May 21st. And Race Officer Pop Parsons was honoured by the award of the Queen's Jubilee Medal. The Sailing Committee also made a presentation to Pop, to mark his 80th birthday.

It was, in fact, quite a year for presentations. The club itself got into the act by deciding to present pennants to its past Commodores, a gesture that was later reported to have been much appreciated by the recipients.

Presentations were also made by Commodore P. N. Harvey to T. C. Weekes and W. C. Roper, both of whom had been members for more than 50 years, and "in appreciation of all the service they had rendered the club in several capacities."

Yet another presentation at about this time was that of a tankard to P. F. Kimmance, who had retired after many years as assistant treasurer.

It was a case of thumbs down though to a ruling by the R.Y.A. that racing flags were no longer necessary. Medway Y.C. decided that as far as it was concerned the flags should be retained.

It was also thumbs down to catamarans, the General Committee confirming that "Cats" were "not acceptable to the club."

There was happier news for the club's Lasers. They were adopted as a sponsored class, with T. Kirby Jnr. elected class captain of a fleet of more than 20 boats.

There were more sailing successes for the club's Wayfarers. W. N. Hodshon won the Eastern Area championship and later shared 1st place with A. J. Wilson in the Western Area championship. In the Eastern Area event Medway competitors D. Kite, P. R. Warner and L. C. Grinter had finished 2nd, 3rd and 4th respectively. Hodshon later went on to finish 5th in the national championships at Torbay.

Security was an ever-increasing cause for concern as the club approached its centenary. There was said to be an abnormal number of cases of theft and vandalism involving boats, cars and trailers. It was even suggested that professional security guards should be brought in to combat the menace.

Eventually it was decided to step up existing voluntary security patrols, in co-operation with the neighbouring Hoo Ness and Upnor clubs, and also to increase outdoor lighting and employ the use of barbed wire on fencing at certain points.

Cruiser members were encouraged to fit burglar alarms to their vessels. A sad reflection, perhaps, of the times in which we live.

CHAPTER THIRTY-THREE

Over and out

Ted Heath, the sailor (centre), seen in jovial mood at the 1977 Dinner and Dance. He had returned specially from Israel to be the club's guest of honour. With him are (from left) Commodore P. N. Harvey, Cllr. Mrs. Daphne MacDonald, Mrs. Harvey, Mrs. Bennett and Mr. A. T. Bennett.

As WE draw towards the close of this long and hopefully enlightening peep behind the M.Y.C. scenes, one question may be engaging the minds of those not entirely familiar with the ways of men of sail. For the benefit of the uninitiated it should be recorded that the sailing season opens in early May and concludes in late October.

What, these unenlightened ones may well be asking themselves, do yachtsmen do with themselves in the winter months? A good question and one that is easily answered.

There is no sailing, of course, but there is still plenty of on-shore activity of one kind or another. The last Saturday of the season is marked by a laying-up party in the clubhouse, usually taking on a fancy dress flavour. One such recent occasion was labelled The Goodies and The Baddies, which must have provided plenty of scope for both dress and characterisation.

The laying-up party marks the start of what can only be described as an interesting and amazingly varied programme of winter events ashore.

Such as a bonfire night party, junior class disco, the annual dinner and dance (with the Joe Loss band, no less), a Christmas party, New Year's Eve supper dance, lectures, class dinners, film evenings, ladies' dinner, men's dinner, knock-out quizzes, the

A.G.M. and Commodore's dinner, various dances, and a bar night in the clubhouse.

A guest of honour at one of the annual dinners had, of course, been that well known sailor-author-politician, Ted Heath, to whom we are indebted for the foreword to this book.

These, and other such occasions lead up to the annual fitting-out party for the season ahead, followed by a new members' evening on the Friday preceding the start of sailing next day, the first Saturday in May.

So, in many respects, Medway is an all-the-year-round club, with so very much to offer its members.

Special mention should perhaps be made of the Fitting-Out Service that is held on the first Saturday of each new sailing season. At the time of writing it is conducted by the Revd. M. G. M. Smith, of Rosherville, Gravesend, who is a club member with his own cruiser, the Shelduck, and who is also the club's official chaplain.

Which is, perhaps, a good note on which to end this Centenary Book. It has been a long and at times arduous task, but one made easier by the friendly co-operation extended from so many quarters.

The research and the writing was always a pleasure and one can only hope that this feeling will be shared, at least in some small measure, by all who do author and club the honour of reading it.

All that now remains to be said is . . . Here's to the next 100 years.

D.E., 1979

Medway Yacht Club burgee.

The distinction of steering the Medway Yacht Club into its second century falls to Commodore N. P. Steele.

The Medway Yacht Club extends its grateful thanks to Mr. Edwin R. P. Boorman, M.A., Managing Director of the Kent Messenger Group of Companies, without whose generous co-operation, this centenary book would not have been possible.

Index

INDEX

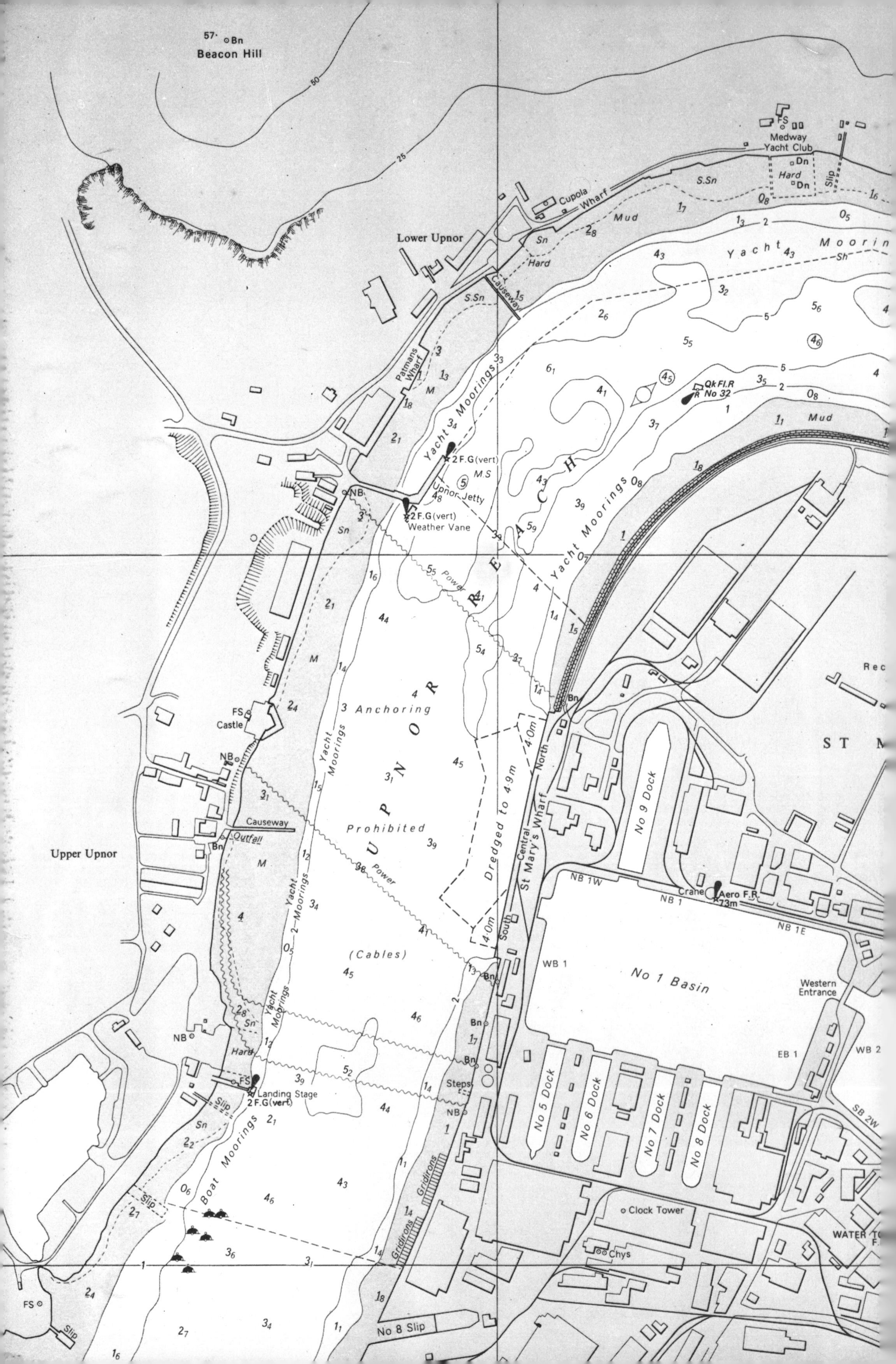

Beacon Hill
Bn
Medway
Yacht Club
FS
Dn
Hard
Dn
Slip
S.Sn
Cupola
Wharf
Mud
Lower Upnor
Sn
Hard
Causeway
S.Sn
Yacht Moorings
Sh
Patmans Wharf
M
Yacht Moorings
Qk Fl.R
No 32
Mud
2 F.G (vert)
M.S
Upnor Jetty
NB
2 F.G (vert)
Weather Vane
Sn
Yacht Moorings
U P N O R   R E A C H
Power
Bn
Anchoring
Prohibited
FS
Castle
NB
Yacht Moorings
Dredged to 4.9m
4.0m
North
Central
St Mary's Wharf
South
4.0m
ST M
Rec
No 9 Dock
Causeway
Outfall
Bn
Upper Upnor
Power
NB 1W
NB 1
Crane
Aero F.R.
73m
NB 1E
Yacht Moorings
(Cables)
Bn
WB 1
No 1 Basin
Western
Entrance
Yacht Moorings
Sn
NB
Bn
Hard
Bn
FS
Landing Stage
2 F.G (vert)
Steps
EB 1
WB 2
Slip
NB
No 5 Dock
No 6 Dock
No 7 Dock
No 8 Dock
SB 2W
Sn
Boat Moorings
Gridirons
Slip
Clock Tower
Gridirons
WATER TO
Chys
FS
Slip
No 8 Slip